GCSE English Literature AQA Anthology

The Study Guide

Poems from
Heaney, Clarke, pre-1914

AQA A Specification — Foundation Level

This book is a step-by-step guide to becoming an expert on the Anthology part of your GCSE English Literature exam.

It's got everything you need to know — annotated poems, exam themes and worked essays.

It's ideal for use as a classroom study book or a revision guide.

What CGP is all about

Our sole aim here at CGP is to produce the highest quality books — carefully written, immaculately presented and dangerously close to being funny.

Then we work our socks off to get them out to you — at the cheapest possible prices.

CONTENTS

Section Four — Themes: Ideas, Attitudes and Feelings

Section Five — Themes: Methods of Poetry

Section Six — How to Answer the Question

☆ = Key poems as suggested by AQA

Published by Coordination Group Publications Ltd.

Editors:
Charley Darbishire, Kate Houghton, Katherine Reed, Edward Robinson, Jennifer Underwood.

Contributors:
Margaret Giordmaine, Roland Haynes, Shelagh Moore, Elisabeth Sanderson, Nicola Woodfin.

With thanks to Kate Houghton, Bert Pringle and Rachel Selway for the proofreading.

ISBN: 978 1 84762 043 9

Groovy website: www.cgpbooks.co.uk
Jolly bits of clipart from CorelDRAW®
Printed by Elanders Hindson Ltd, Newcastle upon Tyne.

How To Use This Book

This book will help you do better in your <u>GCSE English Literature Anthology Exam</u>. It's full of straightforward ways of getting <u>extra marks</u>. Start by asking your teacher which poems and themes you need to study: some schools get you to study all of them, others pick out certain ones.

There are Six Sections in this book

Sections One, Two and Three are about the Poems

There are <u>two pages</u> about <u>each poem</u>. This is what the pages look like:

There's a nice picture of <u>the poet</u> and some info about his/her life.

Important or tricky bits of the poem are <u>highlighted</u> and <u>explained</u>.

Difficult words are defined in the <u>poem dictionary</u>.

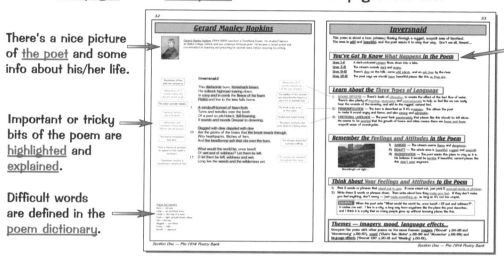

On the right-hand page there are <u>notes</u> about the poem. They include:

• <u>what happens</u> in the poem.

• the <u>language</u> the poet uses.

• the <u>feelings</u> of the poet.

• a bit that will help you to write about <u>how you feel</u> about the poem.

Read through the pages on the poems you've been told to study. When you've read about each poem, <u>shut the book</u> and write out as much as you can remember. See what you've left out, then <u>do it again</u>.

Sections Four and Five are about the Themes

In the exam, you'll have to <u>compare</u> how <u>four poems</u> relate to one of the <u>themes</u>. In Sections Four and Five, there's a page about each of the main themes that might come up. The pages tell you which poems use each theme and how different poets treat the same theme. <u>Read them</u>, <u>understand them</u> and <u>learn them</u>.

Section Six is About Preparing for your Exam

Pages 84-85 tell you how to <u>plan</u> and <u>write</u> good essays using CGP's <u>6-step method</u>. The section also includes <u>exam questions</u> with <u>sample answers</u>. This is what they look like:

Sample <u>exam question</u>.

<u>Sample plan</u> for how you could answer the exam question.

A <u>sample student answer</u>, which continues on the opposite page.

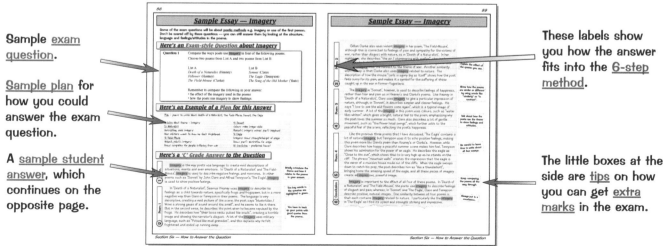

These labels show you how the answer fits into the <u>6-step method</u>.

The little boxes at the side are <u>tips</u> on how you can get <u>extra marks</u> in the exam.

Write some <u>essays</u> using the <u>6-step method</u>. Use the exam-style questions in CGP's foundation-level Heaney and Clarke Anthology Workbook, if you have it, or ask your teacher for some practice questions. You get <u>one hour</u> to answer the question in the exam, so practise doing some <u>timed essays</u>.

Ben Jonson

Key Poem

Ben Jonson (1572-1637) was the son of a clergyman. He attended Westminster School, before becoming a bricklayer and later joining the army. He went on to become one of the most important poets of his time. He also wrote plays and was a friend of William Shakespeare.

The poem is written directly to his son. It's his way of saying a fond goodbye.

He loved his son very much.

On my first Sonne

Farewell, thou child of my right hand, and joy;
My sinne was too much hope of thee, lov'd boy,
Seven yeeres tho'wert lent to me, and I thee pay,
Exacted by thy fate, on the just day.
5 O, could I loose all father, now. For why
Will man lament the state he should envie?
To have so soone scap'd worlds, and fleshes rage,
And, if no other miserie, yet age?
Rest in soft peace, and, ask'd, say here doth lye
10 Ben. Jonson his best piece of poetrie.
For whose sake, hence-forth, all his vowes be such,
As what he loves may never like too much.

His "sinne" was hoping that his son would live for a long time.

Uses money as a metaphor. Jonson's son was "lent" to him for seven years and now he has to "pay" his debt through the death of his son.

Shows his affection for his son.

Says there are advantages of being dead, e.g. you don't have to suffer pain and old age.

His son was his greatest creation.

He decides he'll never love anyone else so much because he doesn't want to feel so much pain again.

This type of language is usually found on a gravestone — the poem commemorates Jonson's son.

POEM DICTIONARY
sinne — an old way of spelling sin
yeeres — years
tho'wert — you were
lament — to feel sorrow or regret
scap'd — a shortened way of writing escaped
miserie — an old way of spelling misery
hence-forth — from now on

On my first Sonne

Key Poem

This is a simple poem about a father who is <u>mourning</u> the death of his seven year-old <u>son</u>. The poem is the father's way of <u>saying goodbye</u> to his son.

You've Got to Know What Happens in the Poem

<u>Lines 1-4</u>	The man says <u>goodbye</u> to his seven year old son who has just <u>died</u>.
<u>Lines 5-8</u>	He says he <u>envies</u> his son because in <u>heaven</u> you don't have to deal with all the <u>horrible</u> things that happen in life.
<u>Lines 9-12</u>	Ben Jonson says that his <u>son</u> was his best ever <u>creation</u>. He decides that in the future he won't <u>love</u> anyone as much as he loved his son so that he won't get so <u>upset</u> if they die.

Learn About the Three Types of Language

1) <u>PRIDE and AFFECTION</u> — The poet is very <u>fond</u> of his son. The poem is written as though he's <u>talking directly</u> to him. This makes it seem very <u>personal</u> and helps you to imagine the poet's <u>feelings</u>.

2) <u>METAPHORICAL LANGUAGE</u> — The poet uses a metaphor about <u>debt</u> and <u>money</u> to describe the loss of his son.

3) <u>COMMENTS ABOUT DEATH</u> — There are quite a few different ideas about <u>death</u> in this poem. On one hand the poet is <u>sad</u> that his son's dead, on the other he says that early death isn't all bad because you don't have to <u>grow old</u> and suffer <u>pain</u>.

Remember the Feelings and Attitudes in the Poem

Rest in Soft Peace

1) <u>GRIEF</u> — The poet is really <u>upset</u> about the <u>death</u> of his son.

2) <u>UNCERTAINTY</u> — The poet <u>wonders</u> whether it is better to be dead than to be alive.

3) <u>PAIN</u> — He's so <u>devastated</u> by his son's death that he decides never to love anyone else as much, because he doesn't want to <u>suffer</u> like this again.

Think About Your Feelings and Attitudes to the Poem

1) Pick 2 words or phrases that <u>stand out to you</u>. If none stand out, just pick 2 unusual words or phrases.

2) Write these 2 words or phrases down. Then write about how they <u>make you feel</u>. If they don't make you feel anything, don't worry — just <u>make something up</u>, as long as it's <u>not too stupid</u>.

> **EXAMPLE** I find it very touching that the poet describes his son as his "best piece of poetrie". Even though he was such a good poet, he thinks that having a son was a greater achievement than his writing.

Themes — death, parent/child relationships, love...

Compare 'On my first Sonne' with other poems about the same themes: <u>death</u> ('Mid-Term Break' p.46-47, 'October' p.62-63), <u>parent/child relationships</u> ('Catrin' p.52-53 and 'The Affliction of Margaret' p.10-11) and <u>love</u> ('Sonnet 130' p.20-21 and 'Mali' p.56-57).

William Butler Yeats

Key Poem

<u>William Butler Yeats</u> (1865-1939) was born in Dublin. He is often considered to be Ireland's greatest ever poet. As well as poetry, Yeats wrote many plays and won the Nobel Prize for Literature. He was also involved in the Celtic Revival, a movement to encourage traditional Irish culture and discourage English influences on Ireland.

Shows the poem is from the point of view of the old mother.

The old woman gets up really early whilst the young people lie about in bed.

Young people only care about unimportant things.

The woman thinks that young people are always moaning.

The woman has no choice but to work.

The poem is in rhyming couplets.

List of all the rubbish jobs that the old woman has to do.

Slow, plodding rhythm suggests the boring, repetitive tasks.

The Song of the Old Mother

I rise in the dawn, and I kneel and blow
Till the seed of the fire flicker and glow;
And then I must scrub and bake and sweep
Till stars are beginning to blink and peep;
5   And the young lie long and dream in their bed
Of the matching of ribbons for bosom and head,
And their day goes over in idleness,
And they sigh if the wind but lift a tress:
While I must work because I am old,
10 And the seed of the fire gets feeble and cold.

The woman gets the fire going in the morning, but by the end of the day it's going out — she'll have to do it all again the next day. This emphasises how boring and repetitive her life is.

The woman's work makes her tired and weak, just as the fire gets weaker as the day goes on.

<u>POEM DICTIONARY</u>
tress — a lock of hair

THIS IS A FLAP.
FOLD THIS PAGE OUT.

William Wordsworth

William Wordsworth (1770-1850) was one of England's greatest poets.
He was born in Cockermouth, and wrote many poems about the Lake District.
He went to Cambridge University. He was made Poet Laureate in 1843.

The Affliction of Margaret

Margaret addresses her son directly in the first stanza.

Where art thou, my beloved Son,
Where art thou, worse to me than dead?
Oh find me, prosperous or undone!
Or, if the grave be now thy bed,

She's desperate to find him, whether he's rich, poor or dead.

She's looking for answers, trying to make sense of her son's disappearance.

5 Why am I ignorant of the same
That I may rest; and neither blame,
Nor sorrow may attend thy name?

Seven years, alas! to have received
No tidings of an only child;
10 To have despaired, and have believed,
And be for evermore beguiled;

Her pain seems to last for ever.

Sometimes with thoughts of very bliss!
I catch at them, and then I miss;
Was ever darkness like to this?

Her lack of knowledge.

15 He was among the prime in worth,
An object beauteous to behold;

She remembers only the best things about him.

Well born, well bred; I sent him forth
Ingenuous, innocent, and bold:
If things ensued that wanted grace,
20 As hath been said, they were not base;

She won't accept any criticism of him.

And never blush was on my face.

Ah! little doth the Young One dream,
When full of play and childish cares,
What power hath even his wildest scream,
25 Heard by his Mother unawares!
He knows it not, he cannot guess:

This fits in with the idea of innocence in the previous verse.

Years to a Mother bring distress;
But do not make her love the less.

She's struggling to control her emotions.

Neglect me! no I suffered long

She knows she's being irrational.

30 From that ill thought; and being blind,
Said, 'Pride shall help me in my wrong;
Kind mother have I been, as kind
As ever breathed:' and that is true;
I've wet my path with tears like dew,

Simile creates an image of gentle but constant crying.

35 Weeping for him when no one knew.

She's suffered on her own.

William Wordsworth

Talks to him directly again.

My Son, if thou be humbled, poor,
Hopeless of honour and of gain,
Oh! do not dread thy mother's door;
Think not of me with grief and pain:
40   I now can see with better eyes;
And worldly grandeur I despise,
And fortune with her gifts and lies.

Nothing but her son matters to her now.

She thinks that birds have fate on their side — but she doesn't.

Alas! the fowls of Heaven have wings,
And blasts of Heaven will aid their flight;
45   They mount – how short a voyage brings
The Wanderers back to their delight!
Chains tie us down by land and sea;
And wishes, vain as mine, may be
All that is left to comfort thee.

50   Perhaps some dungeon hears thee groan,
Maimed, mangled by inhuman men;
Or thou upon a Desart thrown
Inheritest the Lion's Den;
Or hast been summon'd to the Deep,
55   Thou, Thou, and all thy mates, to keep
An incommunicable sleep.

Words of pain and torture — she can only imagine the worst in this verse.

A desperate and irrational way of trying to deal with her situation.

I look for Ghosts; but none will force
Their way to me; 'tis falsely said
That there was ever intercourse
60   Betwixt the living and the dead;
For, surely, then I should have sight
Of Him I wait for day and night,
With love and longings infinite.

Her greatest fear is not being able to talk to him.

She seems to worship him.

My apprehensions come in crowds;
65   I dread the rustling of the grass;
The very shadows of the clouds
Have power to shake me as they pass;
I question things, and do not find
One that will answer to my mind;
70   And all the world appears unkind.

Her worries come to her randomly — she can't control her thoughts.

Her worries have made her weak.

She can't be happy about anything.

Beyond participation lie
My troubles, and beyond relief:
If any chance to heave a sigh
They pity me, and not my grief.
75   Then come to me, my Son, or send
Some tidings that my woes may end;
I have no other earthly friend.

She feels that no one could understand how strong her grief is.

POEM DICTIONARY
affliction — pain
prosperous — rich
undone — ruined
beguiled — fooled
ingenuous — open, honest
ensued — followed
base — bad, corrupt
incommunicable —
    too far away to talk with
intercourse — conversation
betwixt — between
infinite — never-ending
apprehensions — fears
tidings — news

The Song of the Old Mother

In this poem an <u>old woman</u> describes the daily <u>chores</u> she has to do. She seems to think that people in younger generations are a bit lazy and that they have a much easier life than she does.

You've Got to Know What Happens in the Poem

<u>Lines 1-2</u>   The old woman gets up and gets the <u>fire</u> going.

<u>Lines 3-4</u>   She does <u>cooking</u> and <u>cleaning</u> until night time.

<u>Lines 5-8</u>   The woman thinks that <u>younger people</u> (possibly her children) are <u>lazy</u> and that they don't have to do as much <u>hard work</u> as she has to.

<u>Line 9-10</u>   The woman sums up her <u>attitude</u> to <u>life</u>, and the <u>fire</u> she has made starts to <u>go out</u>.

Learn About the Two Types of Language

1) <u>RHYMING COUPLETS AND RHYTHM</u> — the <u>rhyming couplets</u> make the poem sound <u>repetitive</u> like the woman's <u>work</u>. The <u>regular rhythm</u> also makes the poem read like a <u>song</u> which ties in with the <u>title</u> of the poem.

2) <u>CONTRAST</u> — Yeats points out all the <u>differences</u> between the life that the old woman lives and the spoilt lives of the young people.

Remember the Feelings and Attitudes in the Poem

1) <u>SYMPATHY</u> — The poet <u>feels sorry</u> for the old mother.

2) <u>HARD WORK</u> — The poet thinks that the woman's life will <u>inevitably</u> carry on like this until she <u>dies</u>.

3) <u>MORALS</u> — Yeats uses the poem to show people what life is like for <u>old people</u> who have to do lots of <u>work</u> — perhaps he hopes that it will <u>change</u> people's attitudes towards poor elderly people.

Think About Your Feelings and Attitudes to the Poem

1) Pick 2 words or phrases that <u>stand out to you</u>. If none stand out, just pick 2 unusual words or phrases.

2) Write these 2 words or phrases down. Then write about how they <u>make you feel</u>. If they don't make you feel anything, don't worry — just <u>make something up</u>, as long as it's <u>not too stupid</u>.

> **EXAMPLE** The phrase "lie long and dream in their bed" makes me feel sympathy for the woman in the poem and anger towards the lazy young people. The phrase highlights the difference between the lives of the young people and the old woman's life.

Themes — attitudes to others, first person, imagery...

Compare 'The Song of the Old Mother' with other poems about the same themes: <u>attitudes to others</u> ('The Affliction of Margaret' p.10-11 and 'The Laboratory' p.30-31), use of the <u>first person</u> ('Mid-Term Break' p.46-47) and <u>imagery</u> ('Tichborne's Elegy' p.14-15 and 'October' p.62-63).

The Affliction of Margaret

The poet describes the feelings of Margaret, a woman whose <u>son</u> has been <u>missing</u> for seven years. She <u>fears the worst</u>, and she's desperate to talk to him.

You've Got to Know *What Happens* in the Poem

<u>Lines 1-14</u>	Margaret describes the <u>pain</u> of not knowing <u>where her son is</u>.
<u>Lines 15-21</u>	She goes on about how <u>good-looking</u> and <u>well-meaning</u> her son was.
<u>Lines 22-28</u>	She says children <u>don't realise</u> how much their <u>mothers worry</u> about them.
<u>Lines 29-42</u>	Margaret says she was a <u>good mother</u>. She wants her son to <u>return</u>, whatever state he's in.
<u>Lines 43-49</u>	She says that <u>birds</u> have wings, so they're <u>free</u> to return. People <u>don't have</u> this freedom.
<u>Lines 50-56</u>	She imagines terrible things happening to her son, like being <u>imprisoned</u> or <u>shipwrecked</u>.
<u>Lines 57-70</u>	She says it's <u>impossible</u> to talk to the <u>dead</u>. There's <u>no escape</u> from her fears.
<u>Lines 71-77</u>	<u>No-one</u> can understand her grief. Her son <u>returning</u> to her is the only way to end it.

Learn About the *Three Types of Language*

1) <u>OBSESSIVE LANGUAGE</u> — Thoughts of Margaret's son have completely <u>taken over</u> her life. Her thoughts are <u>illogical</u>, and she feels she <u>can't be happy</u> about anything while her son's still missing.

2) <u>PAIN and FEAR</u> — She seems to <u>torture herself</u> by thinking of all the <u>awful things</u> that might have happened to him. She feels that it would be better to know he was dead than not to know anything.

3) <u>REFLECTIVE LANGUAGE</u> — She's sometimes more <u>reasoning</u>, trying to find answers. She feels she <u>can't explain</u> her feelings to anyone — she's <u>alone</u> with her sorrow, and desperate just to <u>talk</u> to her son.

Remember the *Feelings and Attitudes* in the Poem

"I hope he's got some clean underpants..."

1) <u>SYMPATHY</u> — The poet <u>feels sorry</u> for Margaret.
2) <u>ANXIETY</u> — He shows how <u>anxious</u> she is to find out how her son is.
3) <u>DESPERATION</u> — She feels absolutely <u>desperate</u> — nothing matters to her but her son.

Margaret's quite <u>irrational</u> at times — she tries to talk to her son even though he's not there, and her mind jumps from one thought to another fairly randomly.

Think About *Your Feelings and Attitudes* to the Poem

1) Pick 2 words or phrases that <u>stand out to you</u>. If none stand out, just pick 2 <u>unusual words or phrases</u>.
2) Write these 2 words or phrases down. Then write about how they <u>make you feel</u>. If they don't make you feel anything, don't worry — just <u>make something up</u>, as long as it's not too stupid.

> **EXAMPLE** The phrase "I've wet my path with tears like dew" makes me feel really sorry for the mother. It seems there is no end to her suffering, and her pain follows her wherever she goes.

Themes — *parent/child relationship, strong emotions, love...*

Compare 'The Affliction of Margaret' with other poems about the same themes: <u>parent/child relationships</u> ('Follower' p.50-51 and 'Catrin' p.52-53), <u>strong emotions</u> ('The Laboratory' p.30-31 and 'The Field-Mouse' p.60-61) and <u>love</u> ('Mali' p.56-57 and 'Catrin' p.52-53).

William Blake

<u>William Blake</u> (1757-1827) was born in London and educated at home by his mother. He was a poet, artist, engraver and publisher. He believed in the power of the imagination and religion over materialism.

The Little Boy Lost

The boy calls after his dad, but "father" could also mean God.

'Father, father, where are you going?
Oh do not walk so fast!
Speak, father, speak to your little boy
Or else I shall be lost.'

The boy sounds desperate and helpless.

The child seems doomed on his own.

5   The night was dark, no father was there,
The child was wet with dew;
The mire was deep, and the child did weep,
And away the vapour flew.

This could be a ghost leading the boy into danger.

The Little Boy Found

This can be interpreted in different ways. The light could be like the star that led the wise men to the baby Jesus. Or it could be a bad spirit that is leading the little boy into danger.

The little boy lost in the lonely fen,
Led by the wand'ring light,
Began to cry; but God, ever nigh,
Appeared like his father in white.

Suggests God is always there for you when you need him.

God is a much better father to the boy than his actual father.

The boy's mum seems devoted and loving — unlike his dad who failed to look after him.

5   He kissed the child, and by the hand led,
And to his mother brought,
Who in sorrow pale, through the lonely dale
Her little boy weeping sought.

God shows the boy the way home — compare this with line 5 above.

The mother has been crying, just like the boy.

POEM DICTIONARY
mire — mud
vapour — mist
fen — a marshy area
nigh — near
dale — a valley in a hilly area

The Little Boy Lost and The Little Boy Found

These two poems go together to tell a sweet little tale about a little boy who gets lost... and then gets found again, with a bit of help from God. The poems have a <u>religious message</u> — the poet says that God will show us the way when we're lost.

You've Got to Know What Happens in the Poems

The Little Boy Lost

<u>Lines 1-4</u>	A little boy calls out to his <u>dad</u>, asking him to wait so he doesn't get <u>lost</u>.
<u>Lines 5-8</u>	But his dad disappears, leaving the boy <u>lost</u> and <u>crying</u> in the rain.

The Little Boy Found

<u>Lines 1-4</u>	The boy's <u>lost</u> on his own, but luckily for him <u>God</u> shows up.
<u>Lines 5-8</u>	God leads the boy back to his <u>mum</u>, who was out <u>looking for him</u>.

Learn About the Two Types of Language

1) <u>EMOTIVE LANGUAGE</u> — The poet's descriptions of the boy make him seem <u>helpless</u> and <u>vulnerable</u>. This makes the reader <u>pity him</u>. It also shows how he <u>can't cope</u> on his own.

2) <u>RELIGIOUS LANGUAGE</u> — There's lots of <u>Christian imagery</u> in the poem. This supports the overall <u>religious message</u> — that we are <u>lost without God</u>, and can only find safety with his help.

Remember the Feelings and Attitudes in the Poems

These two poems are a bit boring, so here's a picture of something more exciting.

1) <u>FEAR</u> — The boy is <u>desperate</u> and <u>scared</u>.
2) <u>CONCERN</u> — His mother is <u>worried sick</u> about her son.
3) <u>RELIGION</u> — The poet believes people are only <u>safe</u> when they're with <u>God</u>. He thinks people are <u>lost without God</u>.

Think About Your Feelings and Attitudes to the Poems

1) Pick 2 words or phrases that <u>stand out to you</u>. If none stand out, just pick 2 <u>unusual words or phrases</u>.
2) Write these 2 words or phrases down. Then write about how they <u>make you feel</u>. If they don't make you feel anything, don't worry — just <u>make something up</u>, as long as it's not too stupid.

> **EXAMPLE** When the child says "Speak, father, speak to your little boy", I feel really sorry for him. He seems completely helpless and unable to survive on his own.

Themes — danger, strong emotions, imagery...

Compare 'The Little Boy Lost'/'The Little Boy Found' with other poems about the same themes: <u>danger</u> ('The Field-Mouse' p.60-61 and 'Patrolling Barnegat' p.18-19), <u>strong emotions</u> ('The Affliction of Margaret' p.10-11) and <u>imagery</u> ('Storm on the Island' p.48-49 and 'Cold Knap Lake' p.66-67).

Chidiock Tichborne

<u>Chidiock Tichborne</u> (c.1558-1586) was a Roman Catholic. He was part of a plot to murder Elizabeth I and replace her with the Catholic Mary Queen of Scots. The plot was discovered and Chidiock was arrested and condemned to death. He wrote this poem in a letter to his wife, Agnes, just before his death. He was hung, drawn and quartered in 1586, at the age of 28.

Tichborne's Elegy

Written with his own hand in the Tower before his execution

This is supposed to be the best bit of his life.

All these lines are phrased in the same way.

Gloomy language.

The day represents life, the sun represents enjoyment of life.

This line is repeated at the end of the other two verses as well.

My prime of youth is but a frost of cares,
My feast of joy is but a dish of pain;
My crop of corn is but a field of tares,
And all my good is but vain hope of gain.
5 The day is past, and yet I saw no sun;
And now I live, and now my life is done.

The fallen fruit represents his death, the green leaves represent his youth.

My tale was heard, and yet it was not told,
My fruit is fallen, and yet my leaves are green;
My youth is spent, and yet I am not old,
10 I saw the world, and yet I was not seen.
My thread is cut, and yet it is not spun;
And now I live, and now my life is done.

The repetition of "and yet" emphasises the irony of his situation — his life's over, and yet he's still young.

The lines in this verse sound like riddles.

Nearly every word in the poem has just one syllable, making it sound plain and direct.

I sought my death, and found it in my womb,
I looked for life and saw it was a shade;
15 I trod the earth, and knew it was my tomb,
And now I die, and now I was but made.
My glass is full, and now my glass is run;
And now I live, and now my life is done.

Contrast: end of life and beginning of life.

He's convinced he's going to die.

The poem has a regular rhyme scheme.

He hasn't got any hope.

<u>POEM DICTIONARY</u>
elegy — a song or verse commemorating a dead person
tares — weeds
shade — old-fashioned word for a ghost

Tichborne's Elegy

Chidiock Tichborne was about to be <u>executed</u> when he wrote this poem. Unsurprisingly, he's not too chuffed about the idea of <u>dying</u>. Little did he know that he would find everlasting life in the pages of the GCSE AQA English Literature Anthology...

You've Got to Know *What Happens* in the Poem

<u>Lines 1-6</u>   Tichborne contrasts his <u>health and youth</u> with the fact that he's about to <u>die</u>.
                  He uses a series of <u>metaphors</u> to represent his situation.

<u>Lines 7-12</u>   Another verse on the <u>same theme</u>, also using metaphors.

<u>Lines 13-18</u>   This verse is similar to the other two, but this one mentions <u>death</u> directly.
                  All three verses <u>end with the same line</u>, which sums up his fate:
                  "And now I live, and now my life is done."

Learn About the *Three Types of Language*

1)   <u>METAPHORICAL LANGUAGE</u> — Tichborne uses a series of <u>metaphors</u> throughout the poem to make the point that he's really young and healthy, and yet his life's over anyway.

2)   <u>REPETITIVE LANGUAGE</u> — The poem has quite a <u>repetitive structure</u>, e.g. each verse ends with the same line. This emphasises his main point — that he's still young, but is about to die.

3)   <u>LANGUAGE ABOUT DEATH</u> — Death is the main theme of the poem. There's lots of <u>miserable language</u> and imagery about death.

Remember the *Feelings and Attitudes* in the Poem

1)   <u>INJUSTICE</u> — He thinks it's <u>unfair</u> that he should have to die so young — he's being cut off in his prime.

2)   <u>REGRET</u> — He feels <u>sad</u> that's he's got to leave life so soon.

3)   <u>BITTERNESS</u> — There's a tiny bit of <u>bitterness</u> about his situation.

4)   <u>IRONY</u> — It seems <u>ironic</u> to Tichborne that he's about to die even though he's young and he feels healthy.

Think About *Your Feelings and Attitudes* to the Poem

1)   Pick 2 words or phrases that <u>stand out to you</u>. If none stand out, just pick 2 <u>unusual words or phrases</u>.

2)   Write these 2 words or phrases down. Then write about how they <u>make you feel</u>. If they don't make you feel anything, don't worry — just <u>make something up</u>, as long as it's not too stupid.

> **EXAMPLE**   I find the line "And now I live, and now my life is done" very moving.
> The poet knows how hopeless his situation is. Many people in that situation might be
> desperately hoping for escape and freedom, but Tichborne faces his fate. I think this is brave.

Themes — death, irony and imagery...

Compare 'Tichborne's Elegy' with other poems on the same themes: <u>death</u> ('On my first Sonne' p.6-7 and 'Mid-Term Break' p.46-47), <u>irony</u> ('The Man He Killed' p.16-17 and 'Follower' p.50-51) and <u>imagery</u> ('Ulysses' p.26-27 and 'October' p.62-63).

Thomas Hardy

Thomas Hardy (1840-1928) was born in Dorset. He trained as an architect before becoming a very well-known novelist. He wrote classic and often controversial books like 'Jude the Obscure' and 'Far from the Madding Crowd', as well as writing poetry.

The Man He Killed

The whole poem's in speech marks — to make you imagine someone speaking out loud.

'Had he and I but met
By some old ancient inn,
We should have sat us down to wet
Right many a nipperkin!

The 1st and 3rd lines, and 2nd and 4th lines rhyme all the way through.

Informal, friendly language — contrasts with the description of the battle in the second verse.

5   'But ranged as infantry,
And staring face to face,
I shot at him as he at me,
And killed him in his place.

Very simple, straightforward description of dramatic event.

Repetition of 'because' shows he's finding it hard to think of a reason why he killed the man.

'I shot him dead because –
10   Because he was my foe,
Just so: my foe of course he was;
That's clear enough; although

He tries to reassure himself that he was right to kill the man.

Shortened version of "enlist" (to join the army).

Informal language.

'He thought he'd 'list, perhaps,
Off-hand like – just as I –
15   Was out of work – had sold his traps –
No other reason why.

The soldier imagines that the man he killed was similar to himself.

The man he killed was probably a nice bloke who just joined up because he needed a job.

This line is worded almost like it's a joke — but there's a lot of bitterness in it.

Suggests that everyone would do the same thing in a battle situation.

'Yes; quaint and curious war is!
You shoot a fellow down
You'd treat if met where any bar is,
20   Or help to half-a-crown.'

Sounds more like a friend than an enemy.

POEM DICTIONARY
nipperkin — a small amount of beer or liquor
infantry — foot soldiers
foe — enemy
'list — join the army (short for "enlist")
traps — belongings
quaint — odd
help to — lend
half-a-crown — old British coin

The Man He Killed

In this poem, a <u>soldier</u> tells us about a man he <u>killed in battle</u>. He says that even though the man was on the enemy's side, he was probably just a nice, ordinary bloke. He reckons that if he'd met the man in a pub, instead of the battlefield, they might have been <u>friends</u>.

You've Got to Know What Happens in the Poem

<u>Lines 1-4</u>   The soldier says that he could have been <u>friends</u> with the other man, if they had met in an <u>inn</u>.

<u>Lines 5-8</u>   In fact they met in <u>battle</u>, and shot at each other. The other man was <u>killed</u>.

<u>Lines 9-12</u>   The <u>only reason</u> he killed the other man was that they were <u>on different sides</u>.

<u>Lines 13-16</u>   He imagines that the man he killed may have been very <u>similar to him</u> — only enlisting in the army because he needed work.

<u>Lines 17-20</u>   He sums up the message of the poem. He says that <u>war is a strange business</u> — you kill people you might have been friends with in different circumstances.

Learn About the Three Types of Language

1) <u>COLLOQUIAL LANGUAGE</u> — This means <u>informal language</u> that sounds like everyday speech. The poem is written as if the soldier is speaking to the reader.

2) <u>MATTER-OF-FACT LANGUAGE</u> — The soldier uses fairly matter-of-fact language to describe killing the man. This down-to-earth language <u>contrasts</u> with the serious message behind the poem, and helps to highlight the soldier's feeling of <u>bitterness</u>.

3) <u>THOUGHTFUL LANGUAGE</u> — The soldier thinks quite deeply about what he has done. He <u>empathises</u> with the man he killed — he can imagine what it was like to be him.

Remember the Feelings and Attitudes in the Poem

Make friends, not war.

1) <u>IRONY</u> — The soldier has a <u>sense of irony</u> about the situation — he's killed a man he might have been friends with in different circumstances.

2) <u>PUZZLEMENT</u> — It <u>troubles</u> the soldier that the man he killed was probably quite like himself.

3) <u>TRAGEDY</u> — The poet's <u>making a point</u> about the <u>tragedy of war</u>.

Think About Your Feelings and Attitudes to the Poem

1) Pick 2 words or phrases that <u>stand out to you</u>. If none stand out, just pick 2 <u>unusual words or phrases</u>.

2) Write these 2 words or phrases down. Then write about how they <u>make you feel</u>. If they don't make you feel anything, don't worry — just <u>make something up</u>, as long as it's not too stupid.

> **EXAMPLE** The line "Yes; quaint and curious war is!" stands out to me because it's like an emotional outburst. All the way through the poem, the narrator sounds very restrained and matter-of-fact, and then suddenly there is this bitter, sarcastic statement. I can imagine the soldier spitting the words out.

Themes — politics, irony and first person...

Compare 'The Man He Killed' with other poems about the same themes: <u>politics</u> ('At a Potato Digging' p.36-37 and 'The Field-Mouse' p.60-61), <u>irony</u> ('Tichborne's Elegy' p.14-15 and 'Follower' p.50-51) and use of the <u>first person</u> ('Ulysses' p.26-27 and 'Digging' p.44-45).

Walt Whitman

<u>Walt Whitman</u> (1819-1892) was an American poet born in New York. He was one of America's earliest great poets, and was also a teacher and journalist.

Repeated to create a strong first impression of the storm.

An evil sound — dramatic and evil atmosphere.

The poem is one long sentence, with every line ending in "-ing" — this gives a feeling of the storm happening right now, going on and on and on.

Patrolling Barnegat

Onomatopoeia used to describe the noise of the sea.

Wild, wild the storm, and the sea high running,
Steady the roar of the gale, with incessant undertone muttering,
Shouts of demoniac laughter fitfully piercing and pealing,
Waves, air, midnight, their savagest trinity lashing,
Out in the shadows there milk-white combs careering,
On beachy slush and sand spirts of snow fierce slanting,
Where through the murk the easterly death-wind breasting,
Through cutting swirl and spray watchful and firm advancing,
(That in the distance! is that a wreck? is the red signal flaring?)
Slush and sand of the beach tireless till daylight wending,
Steadily, slowly, through hoarse roar never remitting,
Along the midnight edge by those milk-white combs careering,
A group of dim, weird forms, struggling, the night confronting,
That savage trinity warily watching.

Alliteration of "s" suggests the sounds of the waves of the ocean.

Sharp and dangerous, like a sword.

The patrollers fear the worst.

5

10

The beach protects the land from the storm.

Makes the elements sound like an attacking force.

Sounds deep, rough and powerful.

The people in the patrol are hard to see in the confusion and chaos of the storm.

Like sentries on look-out.

Alliteration here sounds like the waves crashing down.

The patrollers face up to the enemy (the storm).

<u>POEM DICTIONARY</u>
Barnegat — a bay in New Jersey, USA
incessant — never-ending
undertone — a hushed sound or voice
demoniac — like the devil
pealing — making a long, loud sound
trinity — three things joined together
combs — the tops of waves
careering — moving quickly
breasting — facing, standing square-on
wending — travelling
remitting — stopping

Patrolling Barnegat

The poet describes a fierce <u>storm</u> blowing at night into a bay in America.
Some people are <u>patrolling</u> the beach, standing up to the wild, cold wind. Brrrrrr....

You've Got to Know _What Happens_ in the Poem

Lines 1-6   A big <u>storm</u> is raging on a beach at night. Strong <u>winds</u> make massive <u>waves</u>
                in the sea which batter the land.

Lines 7-14   Amid the dark and bleak night, people <u>patrol</u> the beach, facing up to the storm.
                They wonder if they can see a <u>shipwreck</u> in the distance (line 9).

Learn About the _Two Types of Language_

1)   <u>WAR-LIKE LANGUAGE</u> — The storm is like a <u>battleground</u> between land and sea.
     The people on patrol on the beach are there to protect the land from attack.

2)   <u>SOUNDS OF THE STORM</u> — There's lots of <u>alliteration</u> and <u>onomatopoeia</u>
     (words which sound like what they're describing). The poet uses these to
     create a sense of the <u>sounds</u> of the howling <u>wind</u> and roaring <u>waves</u>.

Remember the _Feelings and Attitudes_ in the Poem

1)   <u>RESPECT</u> — The poet <u>respects</u> the power of the storm.
2)   <u>ADMIRATION</u> — He <u>admires</u> the bravery of the
     people patrolling the beach.
3)   <u>WARINESS</u> — The people patrolling the beach
     are <u>cautious</u> (line 14).

> There's a sense of <u>dread</u> surrounding the storm
> — the storm seems capable of great destruction.

Think About _Your Feelings and Attitudes_ to the Poem

1)   Pick 2 words or phrases that <u>stand out to you</u>. If none stand out, just pick 2 <u>unusual words or phrases</u>.

2)   Write these 2 words or phrases down. Then write about how they <u>make you feel</u>. If they don't make
     you feel anything, don't worry — just <u>make something up</u>, as long as it's not too stupid.

> **EXAMPLE**   The description of the storm as a "savage trinity" fills me with fear. It sounds like
> a wild animal, with the three forces of the waves, air and night wildly attacking the land.

Themes — nature, danger and language effects...

Compare 'Patrolling Barnegat' with other poems about the same themes: <u>nature</u> ('Sonnet' p.34-35
and 'Storm on the Island' p.48-49), <u>danger</u> ('The Little Boy Lost'/'The Little Boy Found' p.12-13 and
'Cold Knap Lake' p.66-67) and <u>language effects</u> ('Perch' p.38-39 and 'Inversnaid' p.32-33).

William Shakespeare

William Shakespeare (1564-1616) was a successful playwright and poet. He was born in Stratford-upon-Avon, Warwickshire, but lived in London for most of his life. He is one of the most important figures of English literature.

Sonnet 130

My mistress' eyes are nothing like the sun;
Coral is far more red than her lips' red.
If snow be white, why then her breasts are dun;
If hairs be wires, black wires grow on her head.
5   I have seen roses damasked, red and white,
But no such roses see I in her cheeks;
And in some perfumes is there more delight
Than in the breath that from my mistress reeks.
I love to hear her speak, yet well I know
10   That music hath a far more pleasing sound.
I grant I never saw a goddess go:
My mistress when she walks treads on the ground.
　　And yet, by heaven, I think my love as rare
　　As any she belied with false compare.

The word "nothing" changes this line from a compliment into a criticism.

These words might be found in a normal love poem.

Sounds ugly and coarse.

Alternate lines rhyme for the first 12 lines.

These lines start as if they're going to be traditional compliments.

In most love poems, the woman would be compared favourably to these things.

This is the big turning point in the poem. He does love something about her.

He's says he's never seen a goddess, so can't compare her to one.

This woman's real — not some romantic ideal.

The sonnet ends with a rhyming couplet.

Any woman.

This exclamation shows real feeling. He does love her after all.

The last two lines are inset, making them stand out.

POEM DICTIONARY
dun — a brownish-grey colour
damasked — damask roses are a type of sweet-smelling rose, damask is a type of embroidered fabric
reeks — breathes out, smells
belied — misrepresented, shown to be false

Sonnet 130

Shakespeare spends most of the poem seeming to <u>criticise</u> his lover — she's not beautiful, she smells, her hair's all coarse like wire... Then he turns it all around by saying he <u>loves her</u> anyway. You have to hope she was the forgiving sort.

You've Got to Know *What Happens in the Poem*

<u>Lines 1-4</u>	He makes blunt, <u>critical statements</u> about his mistress's looks. She doesn't match up to popular ideas of beauty in Elizabethan times, e.g. she's dark-haired, not fair.
<u>Lines 5-12</u>	He lists other beautiful things (roses, music, perfume, goddesses) but then explains that she <u>isn't</u> like any of these either. On line 9, however, it starts to become apparent that <u>he does like her really</u>.
<u>Lines 13-14</u>	In the <u>final rhyming couplet</u>, he says that he thinks his mistress is <u>great</u> — as good as any other woman who's been praised in love poetry.

Learn About the *Three Types of Language*

1) <u>SUBVERSION OF TRADITIONAL IMAGES OF BEAUTY</u> — Many of the lines sound like they're going to be traditional images of women's beauty. But instead Shakespeare goes <u>against the reader's expectations</u> by saying that his mistress isn't like any of these images.

2) <u>CRITICAL LANGUAGE</u> — He sounds <u>pretty mean</u> about his mistress in the first part of the poem.

3) <u>SONNET FORM</u> — The poem is in traditional sonnet form. It has <u>fourteen lines</u> and is in <u>iambic pentameters</u> (see glossary). Sonnets are often used for <u>love poetry</u>.

Remember the *Feelings and Attitudes in the Poem*

Time for a hair cut.

1) <u>SUBVERSION</u> — Shakespeare's <u>having fun</u> with this poem, turning the reader's expectations of a love poem on their head.

2) <u>CONTEMPT</u> — He sounds pretty <u>insulting</u> about his mistress's looks, voice and smell in the first part of the poem.

3) <u>LOVE</u> — Then at the end, the message seems to be: "I <u>love her</u> warts and all. I don't need to pretend she's a goddess."

Think About *Your Feelings and Attitudes to the Poem*

1) Pick 2 words or phrases that <u>stand out to you</u>. If none stand out, just pick 2 <u>unusual words or phrases</u>.

2) Write these 2 words or phrases down. Then write about how they <u>make you feel</u>. If they don't make you feel anything, don't worry — just <u>make something up</u>, as long as it's not too stupid.

> **EXAMPLE** I really like the phrase "belied with false compare." Often when I read love poetry it does seem pretty false: no one really floats like a goddess or has a voice sweeter than music. The conclusion to this poem is surprisingly down-to-earth and realistic.

Themes — *love, imagery and closing couplets...*

Compare 'Sonnet 130' with other poems about the same themes: <u>love</u> ('Digging' p.44-45 and 'Catrin' p.52-53), <u>imagery</u> ('Tichborne's Elegy' p.14-15 and 'Blackberry-Picking' p.40-41) and a striking <u>closing couplet</u> ('The Village Schoolmaster' p.28-29 and 'Cold Knap Lake' p.66-67).

THIS IS A FLAP.
FOLD THIS PAGE OUT. →

My Last Duchess

In this poem, a Duke is talking to a visitor about a <u>portrait</u> of his wife, who is now dead. He says he really likes the picture, but then he goes on about how she used to <u>smile</u> and have a laugh with everyone, and this annoyed him. We begin to suspect her death may have been a bit <u>suspicious</u>.

You've Got to Know What Happens in the Poem

<u>Lines 1-5</u>	The Duke points out the <u>portrait</u> of the Duchess to a visitor. He's very <u>proud</u> of it.
<u>Lines 5-13</u>	He says people always ask him about the <u>passionate expression</u> on the Duchess's face.
<u>Lines 13-21</u>	The Duke says the Duchess's flirty expression <u>wasn't</u> reserved <u>just for him</u>.
<u>Lines 21-34</u>	He says she <u>smiled at everyone</u>. He's annoyed that she treated him just like <u>anyone else</u>.
<u>Lines 34-43</u>	He says it would have been <u>wrong</u> to <u>criticise</u> her for her behaviour.
<u>Lines 43-47</u>	He acted to <u>stop</u> the Duchess's <u>flirting</u> — but, suspiciously, he doesn't say <u>how</u> he did this.
<u>Lines 47-56</u>	The Duke and his guest <u>walk away</u> from the painting. The Duke reveals he's planning to get <u>married again</u>, this time to the daughter of a Count.

Learn About the Three Types of Language

1) <u>JEALOUS LANGUAGE</u> — The things the Duke says about the Duchess sound quite innocent at first. But we can read <u>hidden meanings</u> into them which hint at the Duke's <u>jealousy</u>, e.g. by saying she <u>smiled</u> a lot, he seems to suggest that she was a <u>flirt</u>, and maybe <u>unfaithful</u> to him.

2) <u>SINISTER LANGUAGE</u> — The Duke sometimes says things that make him sound a bit <u>sinister</u> — there's a <u>dark side</u> to him. We begin to suspect that he might have <u>killed</u> the Duchess.

3) <u>LANGUAGE ABOUT POWER</u> — The Duke feels the need to have <u>power</u> and <u>control</u> over the Duchess. He sees her as another of his <u>possessions</u>, just like his expensive paintings.

Remember the Feelings and Attitudes in the Poem

"The brazen hussy..."

1) <u>PRIDE</u> — The Duke is very proud of his <u>possessions</u> and his <u>status</u>.
2) <u>JEALOUSY</u> — He <u>couldn't stand</u> the way the Duchess treated him <u>no better</u> than anyone else (lines 31-34).
3) <u>POWER</u> — The Duke enjoys the <u>control</u> he has over the painting (lines 9-10). He didn't have this power over the Duchess when she was alive.

Think About Your Feelings and Attitudes to the Poem

1) Pick 2 words or phrases that <u>stand out to you</u>. If none stand out, just pick 2 <u>unusual words or phrases</u>.
2) Write these 2 words or phrases down. Then write about how they <u>make you feel</u>. If they don't make you feel anything, don't worry — just <u>make something up</u>, as long as it's not too stupid.

> **EXAMPLE** When the Duke says "all smiles stopped together", I'm very suspicious of the Duke. His tone suggests he was satisfied with the result of his "commands". As the Duchess is now dead, this seems rather sinister to me.

Themes — attitudes to others, danger and first person...

Compare 'My Last Duchess' with other poems about the same themes: <u>attitudes to others</u> ('The Laboratory' p.30-31 and 'Baby-sitting' p.54-55), <u>danger</u> ('The Field-Mouse' p.60-61) and use of the <u>first person</u> ('The Man He Killed' p.16-17 and 'Death of a Naturalist' p.42-43).

Alfred Tennyson

Key
Poem

Alfred Tennyson (1809-1892) was born in Lincolnshire and later lived on the Isle of Wight and in Surrey. He studied at Trinity College, Cambridge. Tennyson was one of the great poets of the Victorian era and was Poet Laureate from 1850 to 1892.

Alliteration — the harsh "c" sound emphasises the toughness of the eagle and his surroundings.

Strong, determined grip.

Personification — the eagle is described as an old man.

The poet describes the eagle as "he", not "it".

Far away and alone.

Surrounded by a vast emptiness.

He seems to be waiting.

Shows how high the eagle's position is.

The sea looks slow and tame from where he is.

Like a house. The eagle owns the mountain.

Simile shows the eagle's incredible natural power and speed.

Contrast with the end of the first verse. The two sides of the eagle are shown — first waiting, then acting.

The Eagle

He clasps the crag with crookèd hands;
Close to the sun in lonely lands,
Ring'd with the azure world, he stands.

5 The wrinkled sea beneath him crawls;
He watches from his mountain walls,
And like a thunderbolt he falls.

<u>POEM DICTIONARY</u>
azure — blue

The Eagle

Key Poem

The poet describes a magnificent <u>eagle</u>. That's it.

You've Got to Know What Happens in the Poem

<u>Lines 1-3</u>   The eagle stands on a <u>cliff</u>, in front of the sun and surrounded by the big blue <u>sky</u>.

<u>Lines 4-6</u>   The eagle patiently watches the <u>sea</u>, then <u>dives</u> into it for food, quick as a flash.

> Lines 1-3 show how great the eagle looks just <u>standing there</u>.
> Lines 4-6 show how good he looks <u>in action</u>.

Learn About the Three Types of Language

1) <u>PERSONIFICATION</u> — The poet describes the eagle as if it's a <u>person</u> he respects — e.g. he says "him" rather that "it". The eagle is like an admirable <u>old man</u>.

2) <u>LANGUAGE ABOUT ISOLATION</u> — The eagle is <u>alone</u> and <u>unique</u>. He belongs to the <u>sky</u> around him, not the earth way below.

3) <u>POWERFUL LANGUAGE</u> — The eagle is <u>strong</u> and <u>fast</u>. He's the king of everything he sees.

Remember the Feelings and Attitudes in the Poem

"Here, fishy-fishy..."

1) <u>RESPECT</u> — The poet <u>respects</u> the magnificent <u>strong figure</u> of the eagle, perched on the cliff.

2) <u>ADMIRATION</u> — He also <u>admires</u> the physical <u>speed</u> and <u>power</u> of the eagle when he dives towards the sea.

Think About Your Feelings and Attitudes to the Poem

1) Pick 2 words or phrases that <u>stand out to you</u>. If none stand out, just pick 2 <u>unusual words or phrases</u>.

2) Write these 2 words or phrases down. Then write about how they <u>make you feel</u>. If they don't make you feel anything, don't worry — just <u>make something up</u>, as long as it's not too stupid.

> **EXAMPLE** The simile "like a thunderbolt" makes me feel amazed at the eagle's speed. His dive happens in a flash, almost too quick to see, but also with great power.

Themes — nature and imagery...

Compare 'The Eagle' with other poems about the same themes: <u>nature</u> ('Patrolling Barnegat' p.18-19, 'Inversnaid' p.32-33, 'Sonnet' p.34-35, 'At a Potato Digging' p.36-37 and 'Perch' p.38-39), and <u>imagery</u> ('Storm on the Island' p.48-49, 'Mali' p.56-57 and 'A Difficult Birth Easter 1998' p.58-59).

THIS IS A FLAP.
FOLD THIS PAGE OUT.

Ulysses

This poem is about the ancient Greek hero <u>Ulysses</u>. He's returned from the Trojan War to rule his home island of Ithaca as King — but he feels restless. He decides he needs to spend the rest of his life having <u>more adventures</u>. The poem ends with a motivating speech to his crew.

You've Got to Know What Happens in the Poem

<u>Lines 1-5</u>   Ulysses has returned home. He feels <u>frustrated</u> and <u>bored</u> ruling his "savage" people.

<u>Lines 6-32</u>   He decides he has to <u>continue his adventures</u> right up to his dying day. He remembers his past adventures and says there's <u>no point</u> in just sitting about — he has to get all he can out of life.

<u>Lines 33-43</u>   He talks about his <u>son</u>, Telemachus. He says Telemachus is less adventurous, but he'll make a <u>good ruler</u>. Ulysses is proud of him — but he's a <u>different</u> kind of person from Ulysses.

<u>Lines 44-61</u>   Ulysses addresses his <u>crew</u> before they set off on their voyage. He says that he and they may be <u>old</u>, but they're brave and strong men who are still capable of new <u>achievements</u>.

<u>Lines 62-70</u>   Ulysses <u>motivates his crew</u>. He tells them that they're not as strong as they once were, and they may not come back alive, but they're <u>brave men</u> who will give their all.

Learn About the Four Types of Language

1)   <u>HEROIC LANGUAGE</u> — Ulysses proudly describes his exciting <u>adventures</u>. He uses stirring, heroic language to <u>fire up</u> his crew before their next voyage.

2)   <u>IMAGERY</u> — Ulysses creates some <u>powerful images</u> of his battles and adventures.

3)   <u>LANGUAGE ABOUT DEATH</u> — He knows that he's <u>old</u>, and this makes him determined to <u>get the most</u> out of the time he has left. He mentions <u>death</u> several times, but he doesn't seem scared of dying.

4)   <u>LANGUAGE ABOUT FRUSTRATION</u> — He feels <u>bored</u> and <u>frustrated</u> when he's not active.

Remember the Feelings and Attitudes in the Poem

1)   <u>BOREDOM</u> — Ulysses feels <u>bored</u> by the thought of ruling his people at home. He seems <u>scornful</u> of them: "a savage race".

2)   <u>PRIDE</u> — Ulysses is <u>proud</u> of his brave reputation and his great achievements in the past.

3)   <u>EXCITEMENT</u> — He <u>looks forward</u> to the coming voyage and uses his own excitement to <u>inspire</u> his crew.

Think About Your Feelings and Attitudes to the Poem

1)   Pick 2 words or phrases that <u>stand out to you</u>. If none stand out, just pick 2 <u>unusual words or phrases</u>.

2)   Write these 2 words or phrases down. Then write about how they <u>make you feel</u>. If they don't make you feel anything, don't worry — just <u>make something up</u>, as long as it's not too stupid.

> **EXAMPLE**   I really respect Ulysses' courage when he says "my purpose holds / To sail beyond the sunset". This line shows he is determined to continue his adventures for as long as possible, and he is not afraid of death.

Themes — death, memory and first person...

Compare 'Ulysses' with other poems about the same themes: <u>death</u> ('Tichborne's Elegy' p.14-15 and 'October' p.62-63), <u>memory</u> ('Digging' p.44-45 and 'Cold Knap Lake' p.66-67) and use of the <u>first person</u> ('The Song of the Old Mother' p.8-9 and 'My Last Duchess' p.22-23).

Oliver Goldsmith

Oliver Goldsmith (1728-1774) was an Irish playwright and poet. He studied at Trinity College, Dublin. He was also a translator and wrote children's books and histories.

The Village Schoolmaster

Images of the countryside.

There are rhyming couplets all the way through.

Beside yon straggling fence that skirts the way,
With blossomed furze unprofitably gay,
There, in his noisy mansion, skilled to rule,

Describing the school like this shows he was in charge.

It doesn't sound like he was much fun.

The village master taught his little school;
5 A man severe he was, and stern to view,
I knew him well, and every truant knew;

The children were frightened of him.

Well had the boding tremblers learned to trace
The day's disasters in his morning face;

He took his bad moods out on other people.

Full well they laughed, with counterfeited glee,
10 At all his jokes, for many a joke had he:

The pupils pretended to find his jokes funny to keep him in a good mood.

Full well the busy whisper, circling round,
Conveyed the dismal tidings when he frowned;

Sounds like they were scared of his temper.

If he was severe, it was because he liked studying so much.

Yet he was kind, or, if severe in aught,
The love he bore to learning was in fault;
15 The village all declared how much he knew;

He had an impressive range of skills.

There were rumours about him, which suggests no-one knew him all that well.

'Twas certain he could write, and cipher too;
Lands he could measure, terms and tides presage,
And even the story ran that he could gauge.

He was stubborn — he'd carry on arguing even when he was wrong.

In arguing, too, the parson owned his skill,
20 For, even though vanquished, he could argue still;

Suggests he had a loud voice.

While words of learned length and thundering sound
Amazed the gazing rustics ranged around;
And still they gazed, and still the wonder grew

He was an outsider. The villagers didn't know what to make of him.

That one small head could carry all he knew.

Fairly disrespectful way of describing the schoolmaster — the adults weren't scared of him.

He was very knowledgeable.

POEM DICTIONARY
furze — gorse bush
boding — predicting
counterfeited — faked
conveyed — told
tidings — news
aught — anything
cipher — count, do arithmetic
presage — forecast
gauge — measure
vanquished — defeated
rustics — people who live in the countryside

The Village Schoolmaster

This poem is about the old <u>schoolmaster</u> of a village school. He was a rather strange bloke — he was bad-tempered and a bit <u>frightening</u>, but also very <u>intelligent</u> and skilful. Although the poet doesn't say it outright, it seems that the people in the village thought he was a bit of a weirdo.

You've Got to Know What Happens in the Poem

<u>Lines 1-12</u>   The poet points out a place in the <u>countryside</u> where a village school was. Then we hear about how <u>strict</u> the schoolmaster was — he was often in a <u>bad mood</u> and the pupils were <u>scared</u> of him.

<u>Lines 13-24</u>   Then the poet says how <u>clever</u> the schoolmaster was. He had loads of different <u>skills</u>. The villagers were <u>amazed</u> by how much he knew — although they didn't seem to like him very much.

Learn About the Three Types of Language

1)   <u>INTIMIDATING LANGUAGE</u> — The way the schoolmaster looked and acted makes him seem <u>scary</u> and <u>unpleasant</u>. The children were afraid of his <u>temper</u>, and laughed at his rubbish jokes to avoid getting on the wrong side of him.

2)   <u>LANGUAGE ABOUT EDUCATION</u> — The schoolmaster had all sorts of <u>skills</u> and <u>knowledge</u>. The villagers were <u>amazed</u> at how much he knew.

3)   <u>MYSTERY</u> — He was an <u>outsider</u> and a <u>loner</u>. The people in the village didn't know much about him and seemed to think he was a bit <u>odd</u>, rather than respecting him.

Remember the Feelings and Attitudes in the Poem

"Today, children, you're going to learn about how great I am."

1)   <u>FEAR</u> — The children were <u>scared</u> of the schoolmaster.

2)   <u>FASCINATION</u> — The villagers were <u>fascinated</u> by the schoolmaster, but they <u>didn't respect</u> him very much (lines 23-24).

3)   <u>MOCKERY</u> — The poet seems to <u>mock</u> the school master — he suggests he's a <u>pompous show-off</u> (although he doesn't openly say this).

Think About Your Feelings and Attitudes to the Poem

1)   Pick 2 words or phrases that <u>stand out to you</u>. If none stand out, just pick 2 <u>unusual words or phrases</u>.

2)   Write these 2 words or phrases down. Then write about how they <u>make you feel</u>. If they don't make you feel anything, don't worry — just <u>make something up</u>, as long as it's not too stupid.

> **EXAMPLE** The description of the schoolmaster as having "The day's disasters in his morning face" makes him sound scary and intimidating. I wouldn't want to have him as my headteacher.

Themes — memory, attitudes to others, characters...

Compare 'The Village Schoolmaster' with other poems about the same themes: <u>memory</u> ('Blackberry-Picking' p.40-41 and 'Follower' p.50-51), <u>attitudes to others</u> ('My Last Duchess' p.22-23 and 'Baby-sitting' p.54-55) and <u>characters</u> ('The Song of the Old Mother' p.8-9 and 'Catrin' p.52-53).

THIS IS A FLAP.
FOLD THIS PAGE OUT.

The Laboratory

This poem's set in France back in the days when they had a monarchy. A rich woman is buying some poison so that she can kill a woman who is having an affair with her lover/husband (it's not clear exactly who the man is). Seems a trifle extreme...

You've Got to Know What Happens in the Poem

Lines 1-4	The woman talks to the chemist while he mixes the poison in his workshop.
Lines 5-8	Her lover is with another woman and they think she's at church crying — but she's not.
Lines 9-20	She watches the chemist and says how lovely the poisons look. She wants all of them.
Lines 21-24	She plans to poison two other women called Pauline and Elise at the King's Court.
Lines 25-28	She tells the chemist to make the poison brighter, to make her lover's mistress drink it.
Lines 29-32	She says there's not enough poison to kill the mistress — she's too big and strong.
Lines 33-40	Last night, she felt she could kill the mistress by looking at her. She wants her to die painfully.
Lines 41-48	She's so grateful to the chemist she offers to kiss him. Now she's off to use the poison.

Learn About the Three Types of Language

1) VIOLENT LANGUAGE — She's absolutely merciless about taking her revenge. She wants the mistress's death to be horrible and painful, and violent thoughts are never far from her mind.

2) IMAGERY — For all her nastiness, she uses quite fancy language in her descriptions.

3) OBSESSIVE LANGUAGE — She gives up all her wealth and possessions for the poison — nothing else matters to her. She gets very excited when she thinks about revenge.

Remember the Feelings and Attitudes in the Poem

Ice with your poison, I mean drink?

1) OBSESSION — She's obsessed with the thought of getting revenge.
2) SINGLE-MINDEDNESS — revenge is all that matters to her.
3) IMMORALITY — She knows what she's doing is wrong, but she doesn't care.

> She wants to kill the mistress just to get revenge on her lover for being unfaithful — pretty twisted really.

Think About Your Feelings and Attitudes to the Poem

1) Pick 2 words or phrases that stand out to you. If none stand out, just pick 2 unusual words or phrases.

2) Write these 2 words or phrases down. Then write about how they make you feel. If they don't make you feel anything, don't worry — just make something up, as long as it's not too stupid.

> EXAMPLE   I am horrified by the line "He is sure to remember her dying face!". She wants her lover to see his mistress when she dies, which is a very sick way of getting revenge on him.

Themes — death, attitude towards others, strong emotions...

Compare 'The Laboratory' with other poems about the same themes: death ('The Man He Killed' p.16-17 and 'October' p.62-63), attitude towards others ('My Last Duchess' p.22-23 and 'Baby-sitting' p.54-55) and strong emotions ('The Affliction of Margaret' p.10-11).

Gerard Manley Hopkins

<u>Gerard Manley Hopkins</u> (1844-1889) was born in Stratford, Essex. He studied Classics at Balliol College, Oxford, and was a famous Victorian poet. He became a Jesuit priest and concentrated on teaching and preaching for several years, before resuming his writing.

Inversnaid

> Repetition of how dark the stream is.

> Alliteration of "c" sounds makes the stream sound rough.

> Alliteration of "r" sounds suggests the roar of water.

> The bubbles of the stream are described like they're a person's or animal's hair.

This darksome burn, horseback brown,
His rollrock highroad roaring down,
In coop and in comb the fleece of his foam
Flutes and low to the lake falls home.

> The froth is like a hat on the water.

5 A windpuff-bonnet of fawn-froth
Turns and twindles over the broth
Of a pool so pitchblack, fell-frowning,
It rounds and rounds Despair to drowning.

> Constant movement, like a whirlpool.

> Hostile and unwelcoming.

> The stream moves like a person walking.

> Alliteration and repetition shows that there's dew all around.

Degged with dew, dappled with dew
10 Are the groins of the braes that the brook treads through,
Wiry heathpacks, flitches of fern,
And the beadbonny ash that sits over the burn.

> The tree doesn't move but it's alive.

> Repetition gives a passionate, emotional feel.

What would the world be, once bereft
Of wet and of wildness? Let them be left,
15 O let them be left, wildness and wet;
Long live the weeds and the wilderness yet.

> "W" sounds are repeated throughout this verse.

<u>POEM DICTIONARY</u>
burn — stream
coop — an enclosed area
comb — the top of a wave
fawn — light greyish-brown colour
fell — fiercely
degged — sprinkled
dappled — sprinkeld
braes — hills
flitches — cuttings
bereft — deprived

Inversnaid

This poem is about a burn (stream) flowing through a rugged, unspoilt area of Scotland.
The area is <u>wild</u> and <u>beautiful</u>, and the poet wants it to stay that way. Don't we all, Gerard...

You've Got to Know What Happens in the Poem

<u>Lines 1-4</u>	A dark-coloured <u>stream</u> flows down into a lake.
<u>Lines 5-8</u>	The stream sounds <u>dark</u> and <u>angry</u>.
<u>Lines 9-12</u>	There's <u>dew</u> on the hills, some <u>wild plants</u>, and an <u>ash tree</u> by the river.
<u>Lines 13-16</u>	The poet says we should <u>leave</u> beautiful places like this <u>as they are</u>.

Learn About the Three Types of Language

1) <u>SOUND EFFECTS</u> — There's loads of <u>alliteration</u> to create the effect of the fast flow of water. There's also plenty of <u>rhyming</u>, <u>assonance</u> and <u>onomatopoeia</u> (see glossary, p.92) to help us feel like we can really hear the sounds of the country. These effects add to the rugged, natural feel.

2) <u>PERSONIFICATION</u> — The burn is described as if it's a <u>person</u>. This allows the poet to make it sound angry and fierce, and also <u>strong</u> and <u>admirable</u>.

3) <u>EMOTIONAL LANGUAGE</u> — The poet feels <u>passionately</u> that places like this should be left alone. He seems to be <u>worried</u> that the growth of towns and cities means there are <u>fewer and fewer</u> unspoilt areas of countryside.

> Keep an eye out for the <u>compound words</u> (see glossary) in this poem.

Remember the Feelings and Attitudes in the Poem

Something's not right...

1) <u>DANGER</u> — The stream seems <u>fierce</u> and <u>dangerous</u>.

2) <u>BEAUTY</u> — The whole area is <u>beautiful</u>, <u>rugged</u> and <u>unspoilt</u>.

3) <u>PRESERVATION</u> — The poet wants this place to stay as it is. He believes it would be <u>terrible</u> if beautiful, natural places like this <u>didn't exist</u> any more.

Think About Your Feelings and Attitudes to the Poem

1) Pick 2 words or phrases that <u>stand out to you</u>. If none stand out, just pick 2 <u>unusual words or phrases</u>.

2) Write these 2 words or phrases down. Then write about how they <u>make you feel</u>. If they don't make you feel anything, don't worry — just <u>make something up</u>, as long as it's not too stupid.

> **EXAMPLE** When the poet asks "What would the world be, once bereft / Of wet and wildness?", it makes me sad. I live in a city, a long way from anywhere like the place the poet describes, and I think it is a pity that so many people grow up without knowing places like this.

Themes — nature, strong emotions, language effects...

Compare 'Inversnaid' with other poems about the same themes: <u>nature</u> ('Perch' p.38-39 and 'At a Potato Digging' p.36-37), <u>strong emotions</u> ('On my first Sonne' p.6-7 and 'Blackberry-Picking' p.40-41) and <u>language effects</u> ('Patrolling Barnegat' p.18-19).

John Clare

Key Poem

John Clare (1793-1864) was the son of a Northampton labourer. He left school at 11 and educated himself after that. For most of his life he lived in rural Northamptonshire. He is famous for writing poems about life in the country, although he also wrote about politics, the environment, corruption and poverty.

Sonnet

> Repetition emphasises his feelings.

> The soft, fluffy clouds are like wool — a strong visual image.

> Gold and white colours show the brightness of early summer.

> Trees around the lake make it seem alive and healthy.

> Natural and unspoilt.

> The insects are playful and fun-loving.

> Alliteration

> The whole scene is shining brightly.

> Rhyming couplets throughout the poem.

> Gentle movement.

> Brightness continues to the end of the poem.

> The poem finishes on a light-hearted, carefree note.

I love to see the summer beaming forth
And white wool sack clouds sailing to the north
I love to see the wild flowers come again
And Mare blobs stain with gold the meadow drain
5   And water lilies whiten on the floods
Where reed clumps rustle like a wind shook wood
Where from her hiding place the Moor Hen pushes
And seeks her flag nest floating in bull rushes
I like the willow leaning half way o'er
10 The clear deep lake to stand upon its shore
I love the hay grass when the flower head swings
To summer winds and insects happy wings
That sport about the meadow the bright day
And see bright beetles in the clear lake play

POEM DICTIONARY
sonnet — a poem with 14 lines
Mare blobs — buttercups
Moor Hen — a bird that lives on ponds
flag — type of leaf
bull rushes — plants that grow in ponds
o'er — over

At a Potato Digging

Ireland was hit by a <u>Potato Famine</u> in 1845 — a disease called <u>potato blight</u> made the potatoes rot, and thousands of people <u>died</u> from <u>hunger</u>. This poem moves between the modern-day potato harvest, and the Potato Famine.

You've Got To Know What Happens in the Poem

<u>Section I</u>	A description of <u>present day</u> digging and collecting of potatoes.
<u>Section II</u>	A description of the <u>potatoes themselves</u>.
<u>Section III</u>	The <u>Potato Famine</u> — the potato blight and the starving people.
<u>Section IV</u>	A more <u>positive picture</u> of the modern-day workers, having a break.

Learn About the Four Types of Language

1) <u>IMAGERY</u> — There's loads of <u>descriptive language</u> for you to get your teeth into here — like the <u>good potatoes</u> being described as <u>pebbles</u> (line 18) and <u>stone</u> (line 34), making them sound <u>solid</u> and strong, in <u>contrast</u> to the rotted ones during the famine.

2) <u>PAST AND PRESENT</u> — The poet uses a <u>different rhyme scheme</u> for the sections about the present and the past. The poet also uses <u>different tenses</u> to show you where the poem moves between <u>the past and the present</u>.

3) <u>ALLITERATION</u> — There's a lot of <u>alliteration</u> in this poem, e.g. the <u>repeated letters</u> in the second stanza emphasise how the potato diggers are all working together doing a <u>repetitive job</u>.

4) <u>RELIGIOUS LANGUAGE</u> — Heaney makes a lot of religious references in this poem, and refers to <u>Mother Earth</u> and the <u>famine god</u> (lines 12 and 14).

Remember the Feelings and Attitudes in the Poem

1) <u>IRISH CULTURE</u> — The poet sees <u>strong links</u> between potatoes and the Irish, past and present — he feels they're part of their <u>culture</u>.

2) <u>HORROR OF FAMINE</u> — He experiences <u>horror, anger and disgust</u> at the effects of famine, and sees reminders of it in the present.

3) <u>STRENGTH</u> — He appreciates how the Irish have <u>survived</u> the famine, and how they continue to rely on the potato crop, and work hard harvesting it.

Think About Your Feelings and Attitudes to the Poem

1) Pick 2 words or phrases that <u>stand out to you</u>. If none stand out, just pick 2 <u>unusual words or phrases</u>.

2) Write these 2 words or phrases down. Then write about how they <u>make you feel</u>. If they don't make you feel anything, don't worry — just <u>make something up</u>, as long as it's not too stupid.

> **EXAMPLE** The words "putrefied" and "rotted" on lines 35 and 37 make me feel unsettled. They could apply both to the potatoes and to the rotting corpses of the famine victims. The imagery of death and decay in this poem helps me to imagine what the Potato Famine might have been like.

Themes — death, politics and language effects...

Compare 'At a Potato Digging' with other poems about the same themes: <u>death</u> ('On the Train' p.64-65 and 'The Laboratory' p.30-31), <u>politics</u> ('A Difficult Birth, Easter 1998' p.58-59 and 'The Field-Mouse' p.60-61) and <u>language effects</u> ('Perch' p.38-39 and 'Inversnaid' p.32-33).

Perch

Play on words — there are 2 meanings of "perch" on the same line.

The trees cast shadows on the water.

The way the fish flicker about, as well as reminding us of the waves in the water.

Seeing the fish now makes the poet remember watching them in the past.

The river is big and impressive.

Makes the river seem like a house.

The name of a country, but here it means a world full of fishes' fins.

This continues the sentence on the previous line, connecting air and water.

Alliteration and assonance strengthen the idea that the fish look dull and unremarkable.

The fish resist the flow of the river.

Assonance links the blurred movement of the fish with the smooth, air-like rush of water.

Assonance links these 2 words.

Nothing changes between past and present.

Strange grammar gives the impression of continual, flowing movement.

Perch

Perch on their water-perch hung in the clear Bann River
Near the clay bank in alder-dapple and waver,

Perch we called 'grunts', little flood-slubs, runty and ready,
I saw and I see in the river's glorified body

5   That is passable through, but they're bluntly holding the pass,
Under the water-roof, over the bottom, adoze,

Guzzling the current, against it, all muscle and slur
In the finland of perch, the fenland of alder, on air

That is water, on carpets of Bann stream, on hold
10 In the everything flows and steady go of the world.

POEM DICTIONARY
alder — type of tree
dapple — spotted mark
fen — low-lying flat land (often marshland)

Perch

The poet remembers watching <u>perch</u> (a type of fish) swimming in a river when he was younger, and uses this memory to talk about how the world is <u>always moving</u> — but maybe never actually changing. Seamus, they're just fish...

You've Got To Know What Happens in the Poem

<u>Lines 1-2</u>   The <u>perch</u> are described, swimming in the Bann River.

<u>Lines 3-4</u>   The poet remembers how when he was <u>younger</u>, he and others called the perch "grunts". He <u>still</u> sees them now as he saw them in the past.

<u>Lines 5-8</u>   The perch swim <u>against the current</u>.

<u>Lines 9-10</u>   He compares the sight of the fish to <u>comings and goings</u> of the world in general.

Learn About the Three Types of Language

1)   <u>AMBIGUOUS WORDS</u> — Some words are <u>ambiguous</u> — they have <u>more than one meaning</u>, or <u>change their meaning</u> between different parts of the poem. This keeps the reader guessing about what the poem will describe next.

2)   <u>SOUND EFFECTS</u> — There's a lot of <u>assonance</u>, especially between words at the ends of different lines. This <u>links</u> the ideas of different lines together. <u>Alliteration</u> also helps to build up an ongoing effect of the <u>sounds of the river</u>.

3)   <u>PAST and PRESENT</u> — It's sometimes <u>unclear</u> whether what the poet describes is happening <u>now</u> or in the <u>past</u>. The past and present seem to <u>merge together</u> in the poet's mind.

Remember the Feelings and Attitudes in the Poem

"Who are you calling 'runty'?"

1)   <u>FAMILIARITY</u> — Heaney sees the <u>fish</u> as <u>ordinary</u> on the face of it (line 3).

2)   <u>ADMIRATION</u> — He's <u>impressed</u> by the sight of the <u>river</u> (line 4). His descriptions suggest he sees the place as almost <u>magical</u>.

3)   <u>PHILOSOPHY</u> — His <u>memories</u> from when he was younger make him think of how the world keeps on moving <u>all the time</u>, even if we're <u>not aware</u> of it.

Think About Your Feelings and Attitudes to the Poem

1)   Pick 2 words or phrases that <u>stand out to you</u>. If none stand out, just pick 2 <u>unusual words or phrases</u>.

2)   Write these 2 words or phrases down. Then write about how they <u>make you feel</u>. If they don't make you feel anything, don't worry — just <u>make something up</u>, as long as it's not too stupid.

> **EXAMPLE** I find the description of "the river's glorified body" very effective because it makes the river sound like a huge, living being. This phrase reminds me of the River Tweed near my home, which sometimes looks like a body stretching out through the valleys.

Themes — nature, memory and language effects...

Compare 'Perch' with other poems about the same themes: <u>nature</u> ('Death of a Naturalist' p.42-43 and 'Sonnet' p.34-35), <u>memory</u> ('Blackberry Picking' p.40-41 and 'Cold Knap Lake' p.66-67) and <u>language effects</u>, ('Inversnaid' p.32-33 and 'The Eagle' p.24-25).

Blackberry-Picking

Blackberry-Picking

For Philip Hobsbaum

Late August, given heavy rain and sun
For a full week, the blackberries would ripen.
At first, just one, a glossy purple clot
Among others, red, green, hard as a knot.
5   You ate that first one and its flesh was sweet
Like thickened wine: summer's blood was in it
Leaving stains upon the tongue and lust for
Picking. Then red ones inked up and that hunger
Sent us out with milk-cans, pea-tins, jam-pots
10 Where briars scratched and wet grass bleached our boots.
Round hayfields, cornfields and potato-drills
We trekked and picked until the cans were full,
Until the tinkling bottom had been covered
With green ones, and on top big dark blobs burned
15 Like a plate of eyes. Our hands were peppered
With thorn pricks, our palms sticky as Bluebeard's.

We hoarded the fresh berries in the byre.
But when the bath was filled we found a fur,
A rat-grey fungus, glutting on our cache.
20 The juice was stinking too. Once off the bush
The fruit fermented, the sweet flesh would turn sour.
I always felt like crying. It wasn't fair
That all the lovely canfuls smelt of rot.
Each year I hoped they'd keep, knew they would not.

Annotations:

- He talks directly to the reader, to get them involved in the story.
- Strong, intense flavour.
- They were so desperate to collect them that they'd use anything.
- They didn't mind getting wet and dirty — they just wanted the berries.
- This simile makes the berries sound horrible.
- It's gone from delicious to disgusting.
- The start of the poem sounds like an adult talking.
- These words make the blackberry sound sticky and rich, like blood.
- Adult word. The berries create a strong desire for more — it's almost an addiction.
- Juicy and colourful.
- The sounds of these words remind us of the thickness and bright colour of the berries.
- Sounds like the fungus has stolen their food.
- The poet speaks in a child's voice here.
- He gradually realised the sad truth as he grew up.

POEM DICTIONARY
briar — a thorny plant
Bluebeard — a villain in folk stories who murders his wives
byre — a shelter for cows
glutting — eating greedily
cache — a hidden store
fermented — went bad

Blackberry-Picking

The poet remembers picking blackberries when he was a kid. He loved them, and picked loads — but they always went sour pretty quickly. This seems to represent growing up, and learning to accept that sometimes things turn out bad and there's nothing you can do about it.

You've Got To Know What Happens in the Poem

Lines 1-4   The poet describes picking blackberries in summer, when the first few became ripe.
Lines 5-8   The blackberries tasted delicious.
Lines 8-16   He and some others collected loads of blackberries, keeping them in cans, pots and tins.
Lines 17-21 They stored the blackberries in the shed, but they quickly went rotten.
Lines 22-24 It really upset him that the blackberries always went bad.

Learn About the Three Types of Language

1) SENSORY LANGUAGE — The taste, smell and sight of the blackberries is a really strong image. Descriptive words let the reader imagine what the berries are like.

2) CHANGING TONE OF VOICE — The poet is remembering a childhood experience. At the start of the poem, he writes in his adult voice, but at times he uses a more childish tone, especially towards the end of the poem. This lets us see what happens from a child's point of view.

3) METAPHORICAL LANGUAGE — The blackberries are like a hidden treasure. When they go rotten, it's like they've been stolen. The rotten fruit reminds us that good things in life often turn bad.

Remember the Feelings and Attitudes in the Poem

Mmmmmm, blackberries...

1) DESIRE — There's an intense desire to eat the blackberries.

2) DISAPPOINTMENT — As a child, the poet was really upset and angry when the berries went rotten.

3) REGRET — The poet has a tone of regret when he realises that there's nothing he can do to stop the berries, and other nice things, going bad.

> Overall, the tone is fairly calm and thoughtful — but the strong feelings the poet felt as a child are never far away.

Think About Your Feelings and Attitudes to the Poem

1) Pick 2 words or phrases that stand out to you. If none stand out, just pick 2 unusual words or phrases.

2) Write these 2 words or phrases down. Then write about how they make you feel. If they don't make you feel anything, don't worry — just make something up, as long as it's not too stupid.

> **EXAMPLE** The phrase "a rat-grey fungus, glutting on our cache" makes me feel really sorry for the poet. It must have seemed to him, as a child, that some horrible monster had broken in and eaten up his delicious treasure.

Themes — nature, getting older and imagery...

Compare 'Blackberry-Picking' with other poems about the same themes: nature ('Sonnet' p.34-35, 'Inversnaid' p.32-33), getting older ('Follower' p.50-51, 'Mid-Term Break' p.46-47), and imagery ('Mali' p.56-57, 'The Field-Mouse' p.60-61 and 'Patrolling Barnegat' p.18-19).

Death of a Naturalist

Sets the unpleasant atmosphere.

Alliteration creates more atmosphere.

Assonance makes these words stronger and more important.

Sense of 'heaviness', like a hot, lazy summer's day.

Death of a Naturalist

All the year the flax-dam festered in the heart
Of the townland; green and heavy headed
Flax had rotted there, weighted down by huge sods.
Daily it sweltered in the punishing sun.
5   Bubbles gargled delicately, bluebottles
Wove a strong gauze of sound around the smell.
There were dragon-flies, spotted butterflies,
But best of all was the warm thick slobber
Of frogspawn that grew like clotted water
10 In the shade of the banks. Here, every spring
I would fill jampotfuls of the jellied
Specks to range on window-sills at home,
On shelves at school, and wait and watch until
The fattening dots burst into nimble-
15 Swimming tadpoles. Miss Walls would tell us how
The daddy frog was called a bullfrog
And how he croaked and how the mammy frog
Laid hundreds of little eggs and this was
Frogspawn. You could tell the weather by frogs too
20 For they were yellow in the sun and brown
In rain.

Then one hot day when fields were rank
With cowdung in the grass the angry frogs
Invaded the flax-dam; I ducked through hedges
25 To a coarse croaking that I had not heard
Before. The air was thick with a bass chorus.
Right down the dam gross-bellied frogs were cocked
On sods; their loose necks pulsed like snails. Some hopped:
The slap and plop were obscene threats. Some sat
30 Poised like mud grenades, their blunt heads farting.
I sickened, turned, and ran. The great slime kings
Were gathered there for vengeance and I knew
That if I dipped my hand the spawn would clutch it.

Here's that thickness and heaviness again.

Lighter word shows his excitement.

Childish words because he's talking about when he was an infant.

Military word.

First time it's about the poet, not the dam.

These words are like the ones in lines 1-10. It's hot and sticky again.

Military word.

Disgusting images — suggest foulness.

Military word.

Alliteration strengthens the words and the atmosphere created.

Onomatopoeia strengthens the atmosphere.

This is a simile.

Military word.

This is a metaphor.

These images show the boy's fear.

POEM DICTIONARY
Naturalist — someone who is interested in nature
flax — plant with blue flowers that is usually grown for thread for cloth, and for its seed (flaxseed).
festered — rotted
coarse — rough, unpleasant
cocked — ready to fire, like a gun
sods — pieces of turf
obscene — disgusting
poised — ready for action
vengeance — revenge

Section Two — Seamus Heaney

Death of a Naturalist

Key Poem

In this one, the poet (still that Irish fella Seamus Heaney) writes about <u>frogs and frogspawn</u>. It's about when his feelings towards them changed. At first he was <u>fascinated</u> by them. But <u>later</u> the sight of grown frogs at a dam where he used to play made him <u>scared</u>.

You've Got To Know *What Happens* in the Poem

Lines 1-10   The <u>flax-dam</u> is described (a dam in a river, made of the plant flax).

Lines 10-15   These talk about the <u>poet's enthusiasm</u> and excitement for the frogs and the dam.

Lines 15-21   These are about the infant <u>teacher's fairy-story approach</u> to it all.

Line 21   This is where the <u>change happens</u>. The change is emphasised by the words "In rain" being on their own, and a new stanza beginning.

Lines 22-30   These describe the poet discovering the <u>scary adult frogs</u>.

Lines 31-33   These describe the <u>poet's disgust and fear</u>.

Learn About the *Three Types of Language*

1) <u>SENSORY LANGUAGE</u> — This describes things you can touch, see, smell or hear. These make it all seem <u>more real</u> in your head (e.g. "<u>festered</u>" and "<u>gargled</u>").

2) <u>CHILDISH LANGUAGE</u> — This is used when the poet is talking about <u>childhood</u>. He uses long, <u>rambling sentences</u>, and words like "<u>daddy</u>" and "<u>mammy</u>".

3) <u>MILITARY LANGUAGE</u> — This is used when the poet sees the frogs enter the dam. They're now <u>scary like war</u>, not funny and innocent, like when he was young. (E.g. "<u>grenades</u>", "<u>threats</u>").

Remember the *Feelings and Attitudes* in the Poem

1) <u>MEMORY</u> — This poem is a <u>memory</u> of his <u>feelings</u> as a young boy.

2) <u>EXCITEMENT</u> — At first he's <u>excited</u> by the frogspawn (lines 8-10).

3) <u>FEAR</u> — Later, the boy is <u>frightened by the frogs</u> taking over the flax-dam (lines 31-33).

4) <u>SIGNIFICANCE</u> — The poet, Seamus Heaney, looks back on this moment in his life as making a <u>significant impact on his personality</u>.

> This poem is also about growing up. The poet sees the frogs differently from when he was in infants.

Think About *Your Feelings and Attitudes* to the Poem

1) Pick 2 words or phrases that <u>stand out to you</u>. If none stand out, just pick 2 <u>unusual words or phrases</u>.

2) Write these 2 words or phrases down. Then write about how they <u>make you feel</u>. If they don't make you feel anything, don't worry — just <u>make something up</u>, as long as it's not too stupid.

> **EXAMPLE**   The phrase on line 30 about the frogs, "their blunt heads farting", sounds disgusting and makes me feel sick. The phrase is very effective in helping the reader sympathise with the feelings of the character in the poem.

Themes — nature, getting older and first person...

Compare 'Death of a Naturalist' with other poems about the same themes: <u>nature</u> ('Blackberry-Picking' p.40-41 and 'Inversnaid' p.32-33), <u>getting older</u> ('Follower' p.50-51) and use of the <u>first person</u> ('On the Train' p.64-65, 'Cold Knap Lake' p.66-67 and 'The Man He Killed' p.16-17).

Key Poem

Digging

Digging

Between my finger and my thumb
The squat pen rests; snug as a gun.

> This is assonance — the 'u' is repeated. The short, sharp effect is like the noise of digging.

> This makes the pen sound ugly.

Under my window, a clean rasping sound
When the spade sinks into the gravelly ground:
5   My father, digging. I look down

> Alliteration.

Till his straining rump among the flowerbeds
Bends low, comes up twenty years away
Stooping in rhythm through potato drills
Where he was digging.

> As the poet watches his father digging, it brings back memories of him digging potatoes twenty years ago.

10   The coarse boot nestled on the lug, the shaft
Against the inside knee was levered firmly.
He rooted out tall tops, buried the bright edge deep
To scatter new potatoes that we picked
Loving their cool hardness in our hands.

> He's describing how they felt to touch.

> The alliteration gives a digging rhythm.

15   By God, the old man could handle a spade.
Just like his old man.

> This exclamation really stands out. It's as if the poet has said it out loud.

My grandfather cut more turf in a day
Than any other man on Toner's bog.
Once I carried him milk in a bottle
20   Corked sloppily with paper. He straightened up
To drink it, then fell to right away

> These memories also remind him of his grandfather digging.

> This shows the family pride in digging — his grandfather was the best at it.

> His grandfather was so absorbed in digging that he got straight back to work.

Nicking and slicing neatly, heaving sods
Over his shoulder, going down and down
For the good turf. Digging.

> These verbs mimic the sound of a spade digging.

25   The cold smell of potato mould, the squelch and slap
Of soggy peat, the curt cuts of an edge
Through living roots awaken in my head.
But I've no spade to follow men like them.

> Onomatopoeia

> Alliteration

> The poet hasn't inherited this skill.

Between my finger and my thumb
30   The squat pen rests.
I'll dig with it.

> This image is repeated from the first stanza.

> The poet links writing and digging. He uses his pen like a spade, to dig out memories and ideas.

POEM DICTIONARY
squat — short and wide
coarse — rough
sods — pieces of turf
curt — short

Digging

Key Poem

The poet is inside writing while his <u>father</u> digs the garden. The sight reminds him of seeing his father digging potatoes and his <u>grandfather</u> digging peat in the past. He isn't following in their footsteps, but he does "dig" out ideas with his pen.

You've Got To Know What Happens in the Poem

<u>Lines 1-6</u>	The poet is sitting <u>inside</u>, <u>writing</u>, and watching his father <u>digging outside</u>.
<u>Lines 7-24</u>	The poet describes his <u>memories</u> of his <u>father</u> and his <u>grandfather</u>, digging.
<u>Lines 25-27</u>	The poet describes his <u>memories</u> of what <u>digging</u> felt like.
<u>Lines 28-31</u>	The poet goes back to describe what he does as a <u>writer</u>, and links this to the idea of <u>digging</u>.

Learn About the Three Types of Language

1) <u>REFERENCES TO MEMORIES AND FEELINGS</u> — The poet is watching his father digging in the flowerbed in the <u>present</u>. This brings back <u>memories</u> of his father digging potatoes, and his <u>grandfather</u> digging peat. The poet shows the <u>pride</u> he feels in their skill and hard work.

2) <u>DESCRIPTIVE LANGUAGE</u> — The poet uses <u>alliteration</u> to give the poem the <u>rhythm</u> of someone digging. The verbs he uses are very clean, <u>sharp-sounding</u> phrases, like "<u>rooted out</u>", "<u>nicking and slicing</u>".

3) <u>THE POET'S THOUGHTS</u> — Most of the poem is description, but there are a few lines where the poet writes down his thoughts more <u>directly</u>. These are particularly <u>effective</u> because of the way they break up the description, and because at the end of the poem the poet <u>realises</u> that his own skill is important too.

Remember the Feelings and Attitudes in the Poem

"I'm sure I buried it round here somewhere..."

1) <u>RESPECT</u> — The poet feels <u>respect</u> for his father and grandfather.

2) <u>GUILT</u> — He also feels <u>guilty</u> that he hasn't followed in their footsteps.

3) <u>MEMORIES</u> — He's got <u>fond memories</u> of his past.

Think About Your Feelings and Attitudes to the Poem

1) Pick 2 words or phrases that <u>stand out to you</u>. If none stand out, just pick 2 <u>unusual words or phrases</u>.

2) Write these 2 words or phrases down. Then write about how they <u>make you feel</u>. If they don't make you feel anything, don't worry — just <u>make something up</u>, as long as it's not too stupid.

> **EXAMPLE** The phrases "cold smell of potato mould" and "squelch and slap / Of soggy peat" really bring to life the smells and sounds of digging in wet and muddy earth. It reminds me of the feeling of earth on my hands, which always makes me feel really cold, wet and dirty.

Themes — memory, parent/child relationships, characters...

Compare 'Digging' with other poems about the same themes: <u>memory</u> ('Cold Knap Lake' p.66-67 and 'Follower' p.50-51), <u>parent/child relationships</u> ('Mali' p.56-57 and 'The Affliction of Margaret' p.10-11) and strong <u>characters</u> ('Catrin' p.52-53 and 'The Village Schoolmaster' p.28-29).

Section Two — Seamus Heaney

Mid-Term Break

Mid-Term Break

I sat all morning in the college sick bay
Counting bells knelling classes to a close.
At two o'clock our neighbours drove me home.

5 In the porch I met my father crying—
He had always taken funerals in his stride—
And Big Jim Evans saying it was a hard blow.

The baby cooed and laughed and rocked the pram
When I came in, and I was embarrassed
By old men standing up to shake my hand

10 And tell me they were "sorry for my trouble".
Whispers informed strangers I was the eldest,
Away at school, as my mother held my hand

In hers and coughed out angry tearless sighs.
At ten o'clock the ambulance arrived
15 With the corpse, stanched and bandaged by the nurses.

Next morning I went up into the room. Snowdrops
And candles soothed the bedside; I saw him
For the first time in six weeks. Paler now,

Wearing a poppy bruise on his left temple,
20 He lay in the four foot box as in his cot.
No gaudy scars, the bumper knocked him clear.

A four foot box, a foot for every year.

Annotations:

- Using the exact time makes the poem sound very factual.
- You can tell this is a very sad event because he says it's unusual to see his father crying, even at a funeral.
- This contrasts with his dead brother in lines 18-21.
- He's embarrassed by the reactions of other people.
- They're talking about the poet as if he wasn't there.
- Compare his mother's emotions to those of his father in line 4.
- Assonance
- The time makes these events seem very matter-of-fact.
- The candles and snowdrops are part of the grieving process. They're personified here.
- Remember the title of the poem — the poet has been away at school until now.
- This is very descriptive, in contrast to most of the poem.
- This contrasts with the living baby in line 7.
- "Gaudy" doesn't fit with the word "scars" — it's usually a cheerful word. This makes it stand out.
- There's no emotion in this phrase, even though it describes a terrible accident.
- Repeating the numbers emphasises the tiny coffin, and we realise for the first time how young his brother was.
- This is the only rhyme in the poem, which adds to the impact of the last line.

POEM DICTIONARY
knelling — the sound of bells ringing, usually for a funeral
stanched — made to stop bleeding
gaudy — horribly bright

Section Two — Seamus Heaney

Mid-Term Break

This poem is about Heaney's memories of his brother's funeral. He comes home from boarding school and has to face the reactions of his family and neighbours, and see the corpse.

You've Got To Know What Happens in the Poem

Lines 1-3	He's at school waiting to be taken home.
Lines 4-13	He arrives home for the funeral and faces the reactions of his family and the other mourners.
Lines 14-15	His brother's body is brought home.
Lines 16-22	He goes to see his brother's body in the coffin.

Learn About the Three Types of Language

1) IMAGERY — The poem is very factual. So when the poet does use imagery, it really stands out, e.g. when he uses the phrase "poppy bruise" to describe his brother's wound.

2) DESCRIPTIONS OF PEOPLE'S REACTIONS — Heaney describes the reactions of "strangers" and of his family to the death. The detached descriptions help you to imagine the numbness he might have felt at the time, and how he was embarrassed by the attention he received.

3) REFERENCES TO TIME — There are several references to time, and time passing in this poem. This gives the impression of going through a ritual, but it also gives a sense of how time has stopped for the dead boy, especially in the last line, "a foot for every year" — he won't get any taller, or any older.

Remember the Feelings and Attitudes in the Poem

1) GRIEF — The poet is remembering his past grief.

2) ADOLESCENCE — As a boy he is embarrassed by the reactions of others.

3) SHOCK — There's a sense of being shocked and stunned when he views the corpse, and the feeling of everything stopping for the dead child.

4) RITUAL — He sees the importance of ritual in the grieving process, e.g. "Snowdrops / And candles soothed the bedside", and the fact that a terrible event still has a routine.

Think About Your Feelings and Attitudes to the Poem

1) Pick 2 words or phrases that stand out to you. If none stand out, just pick 2 unusual words or phrases.

2) Write these 2 words or phrases down. Then write about how they make you feel. If they don't make you feel anything, don't worry — just make something up, as long as it's not too stupid.

> **EXAMPLE** The phrases "The baby cooed and laughed and rocked the pram" and "He lay... as in his cot" make me feel really sad. The contrast between the baby and Heaney's dead brother seems worse when you realise his brother was young enough to sleep in a cot.

Themes — death, getting older and strong emotions...

Compare 'Mid-Term Break' with other poems about the same themes: death ('October' p.62-63 and 'On my first Sonne' p.6-7), getting older ('Blackberry-Picking' p.40-41 and 'Death of a Naturalist' p.42-43) and strong emotions ('Catrin' p.52-53 and 'The Field-Mouse' p.60-61).

Storm on the Island

Storm on the Island

We are prepared: we build our houses squat,
Sink walls in rock and roof them with good slate.
The wizened earth has never troubled us
With hay, so, as you can see, there are no stacks
5 Or stooks that can be lost. Nor are there trees
Which might prove company when it blows full
Blast: you know what I mean – leaves and branches
Can raise a tragic chorus in a gale
So that you can listen to the thing you fear
10 Forgetting that it pummels your house too.
But there are no trees, no natural shelter.
You might think that the sea is company,
Exploding comfortably down on the cliffs
But no: when it begins, the flung spray hits
15 The very windows, spits like a tame cat
Turned savage. We just sit tight while wind dives
And strafes invisibly. Space is a salvo.
We are bombarded by the empty air.
Strange, it is a huge nothing that we fear.

This is a very strong, safe opening statement. Compare it to the last line of the poem.

Nothing grows there.

This is a metaphor — trees sound like they're wailing or singing.

This is an unusual combination of words, mixing the ideas of fear and safety.

This is language normally used to describe war.

There's a lot of words about safety and security in the first two lines.

This is the first hint of fear in the poem — why are there no crops on the island?

The word "company" is used here and on line 12, to emphasise the loneliness.

The poem seems more scary because the poet is talking directly to you.

This is a very violent way to describe the wind.

This simile shows how familiar things become frightening during the storm.

All they can do is wait helplessly for the storm to end.

The storm is invisible, there's nothing solid there. This contrasts with the solid rock mentioned in the first two lines of the poem.

POEM DICTIONARY
wizened — dried up
stooks — piles of sheaves (bundles) of corn
strafes — attacks with gunfire at close range, often from the air
salvo — lots of guns firing at once

Storm on the Island

This poem describes the effects of a fierce <u>storm</u> on the inhabitants of an island.
They <u>prepare</u> for the storm, but once it starts, they feel <u>scared</u> anyway...

You've Got To Know What Happens in the Poem

<u>Lines 1-5</u>	The community thinks it is <u>prepared</u> for the storm.
<u>Lines 6-13</u>	This is where the poem starts to <u>change</u> from security to fear. It describes the power and the sounds of the storm itself.
<u>Lines 14-19</u>	This part describes the <u>fear</u> as the storm attacks the island.

Learn About the Three Types of Language

1) <u>CONTRASTING DESCRIPTIONS OF SAFETY AND FEAR</u> — The poem uses a lot of words to do with <u>safety</u> and <u>security</u> at the beginning of the poem. The tone changes though, and the sense of <u>loneliness</u> increases as <u>familiar</u> things become <u>frightening</u> during the storm.

2) <u>DIRECT TONE</u> — The poet involves you in his fear of the storm by speaking <u>directly</u> to "you", the reader.

3) <u>IMAGERY</u> — The poet creates <u>word pictures</u> of the storm using <u>descriptive language</u>, e.g. he uses the type of language normally used to describe <u>war</u>, to emphasise the violence of the storm.

Remember the Feelings and Attitudes in the Poem

1) <u>SAFETY</u> — The first part of the poem shows the community's feelings of <u>safety</u>, and <u>preparation</u> for the storm.

2) <u>FEAR</u> — This sense of security soon changes to <u>fear</u>, as familiar things <u>change</u> and become <u>frightening</u>.

3) <u>HELPLESSNESS</u> — The people can't do anything about their fear except wait for the storm to finish. This is a strong <u>contrast</u> to the start of the poem.

> The first eight letters of the title spell STORMONT. Stormont Castle is an important location for Northern Irish politics. You could link the themes of fear and safety in this poem with the Northern Ireland conflict.

Think About Your Feelings and Attitudes to the Poem

1) Pick 2 words or phrases that <u>stand out to you</u>. If none do, just pick 2 <u>unusual words or phrases</u>.

2) Write these 2 words or phrases down. Then write about how they <u>make you feel</u>. If they don't make you feel anything, don't worry — just <u>make something up</u>, as long as it's not too stupid.

> **EXAMPLE** The contrast between the phrase "We are prepared" and "it is a huge nothingness that we fear" makes me feel frightened. The confidence of the first few lines has been replaced at the end of the poem by fear of a frightening, invisible force.

Themes — nature, danger and imagery...

Compare 'Storm on the Island' with other poems about the same themes: <u>nature</u> ('Inversnaid' p.32-33 and 'Perch' p.38-39), <u>danger</u> ('The Little Boy Lost'/'The Little Boy Found' p.12-13 and 'Patrolling Barnegat p.18-19) and <u>imagery</u> ('October' p.62-63 and 'At a Potato Digging' p.36-37).

Follower

Follower

My father worked with a horse-plough,
His shoulders globed like a full sail strung
Between the shafts and the furrow.
The horses strained at his clicking tongue.

5   An expert. He would set the wing
And fit the bright steel-pointed sock.
The sod rolled over without breaking.
At the headrig, with a single pluck

Of reins, the sweating team turned round
10 And back into the land. His eye
Narrowed and angled at the ground,
Mapping the furrow exactly.

I stumbled in his hob-nailed wake,
Fell sometimes on the polished sod;
15 Sometimes he rode me on his back
Dipping and rising to his plod.

I wanted to grow up and plough,
To close one eye, stiffen my arm.
All I ever did was follow
20 In his broad shadow round the farm.

I was a nuisance, tripping, falling,
Yapping always. But today
It is my father who keeps stumbling
Behind me, and will not go away.

Simile.

This suggests tough, physical work

This shows his father's level of skill and control.

This sounds a bit like someone navigating a ship

The poet found it hard to follow in his father's footsteps.

In line 13 the boy was stumbling behind his father. Now the roles are reversed.

"Rolled" and "breaking" suggest waves of the sea.

This shows how skilled his father is.

The horses pulling the plough.

Uses language of the sea and sailing.

The regular rhythm of this line emphasises the child's movement on his father's back.

Each stanza has at least two lines which rhyme.

He felt unable to keep up with his father.

POEM DICTIONARY
globed — rounded (like a globe)
shafts — wooden poles which harness the animal to the plough
furrow — a long narrow trench made by the plough in the soil
wing — part of the frame of the plough
sock — the end of the plough that cuts the soil
headrig — the end of the ploughed part of the field where the horse has to turn round (also part of a ship's rigging)
hob-nailed — hob-nailed boots are heavy work shoes
sod — grass covered earth

Follower

The poet remembers being a young boy following his father as he did the <u>ploughing</u>. Now he's older, he says the roles have reversed — his <u>father follows him instead</u>. He might mean that his father is now old and dependent. Or he might mean that his father is dead, and the memories won't go away.

You've Got To Know What Happens in the Poem

<u>Lines 1-12</u>	These lines describe the father's <u>expert</u> ploughing.
<u>Lines 13-16</u>	The narrator <u>followed his father</u> round the farm. Sometimes his father gave him a piggy-back.
<u>Lines 17-22</u>	These describe the narrator's sense of <u>failure</u> — he wanted to be like his father, but all he ever did was follow him around being a <u>nuisance</u>.
<u>Lines 23-24</u>	Now they're older, the relationship has been <u>reversed</u>, and now his <u>father</u> is the <u>follower</u>.

Learn About the Three Types of Language

1) <u>SAILING IMAGERY</u> — The poet uses images of sailing and the <u>sea</u> to show how his father looked when he was ploughing, e.g. "<u>without breaking</u>" likens the ploughed earth to <u>waves</u> on the sea.

2) <u>LANGUAGE SHOWING SKILL AND CONTROL</u> — The poet emphasises the skill his father had, controlling the straining horses with his "<u>clicking tongue</u>". This shows the <u>admiration</u> he felt for his father.

3) <u>REFLECTIVE LANGUAGE</u> — The poet sees himself through his father's eyes, as a "<u>nuisance</u>", and maybe a failure, but this is <u>reversed</u> in the last stanza, where his father is the one "stumbling / Behind".

Remember the Feelings and Attitudes in the Poem

Geoff dreamed of being a Roman chariot-racer.

1) <u>ADMIRATION</u> — The poet <u>admires</u> his father's skill at ploughing.

2) <u>HERO-WORSHIP</u> — As a child, he <u>struggled</u> to follow his father and <u>hoped</u> to take his place one day.

3) <u>FEELINGS OF FAILURE</u> — The poet worries that he is a <u>failure</u> because he didn't follow in his father's footsteps.

4) <u>FAMILY TIES</u> — The poet's relationship with his father is <u>still important</u> to him now that he's <u>older</u> — it "will not go away".

Think About Your Feelings and Attitudes to the Poem

1) Pick 2 words or phrases that <u>stand out to you</u>. If none do, just pick 2 <u>unusual words or phrases</u>.

2) Write these 2 words or phrases down. Then write about how they <u>make you feel</u>. If they don't make you feel anything, don't worry — just <u>make something up</u>, as long as it's not too stupid.

> **EXAMPLE** The phrase "single pluck" shows how skilful the poet's father was at ploughing with horses. The phrase sounds like a sharp, sudden movement, which is emphasised by putting it at the end of the stanza. It makes me admire his father's skill, and understand why the poet wanted to be like him.

Themes — parent/child relationships, memory, characters...

Compare 'Follower' with other poems about the same themes: <u>parent/child relationships</u> ('Digging' p.44-45 and 'Catrin' p.52-53), <u>memory</u> ('Perch' p.38-39 and 'Cold Knap Lake' p.66-67) and strong <u>characters</u> ('Mid-Term Break' p.46-47 and 'The Song of the Old Mother' p.8-9).

Key Poem

Catrin

Gillian Clarke was born in 1937 in Cardiff. In 1990 she co-founded a writers' centre in North Wales called Ty Newydd. She teaches creative writing at the University of Glamorgan. Many of her poems reflect her cultural identity and family relationships in Wales.

Catrin

> The poet is talking directly to her daughter.

> Before the birth, life was ordinary and peaceful.

I can remember you, child,
As I stood in a hot, white
Room at the window watching
The people and cars taking
5   Turn at the traffic lights.

> She and her daughter were fighting each other even before she was born.

I can remember you, our first
Fierce confrontation, the tight
Red rope of love which we both
Fought over. It was a square

> They are in competition with each other.

10 Environmental blank, disinfected
Of paintings or toys. I wrote
All over the walls with my

> The shouts of pain fill the bare, simple room with emotion.

Words, coloured the clean squares
With the wild, tender circles

> Suggests affection between parent and child.

15 Of our struggle to become
Separate. We want, we shouted,
To be two, to be ourselves.

> They both want to be separated.

> Being on a separate line shows the importance of this word.

Neither won nor lost the struggle
In the glass tank clouded with feelings
20 Which changed us both. Still I am fighting
You off, as you stand there

> Years later, they still haven't broken free from each other.

> She admires her daughter's strength and beauty.

With your straight, strong, long
Brown hair and your rosy,
Defiant glare, bringing up
25 From the heart's pool that old rope,
Tightening about my life,
Trailing love and conflict,

> The rope stands for her struggle with her daughter — and the mixed emotions of love and conflict this brings up.

As you ask may you skate
In the dark, for one more hour.

POEM DICTIONARY
disinfected — cleaned

Catrin

Key Poem

In this poem, the poet talks to her <u>daughter</u>. She describes the struggle of the <u>birth</u>, and says that they're <u>still struggling</u> with each other years later. Like, guys, get over it ok...

You've Got To Know What Happens in the Poem

Lines 1-9 — The poet tells her <u>daughter</u> about when she was born. She remembers staring out of the <u>window</u> (lines 1-5), before the difficulties of the <u>birth</u> (6-9).

Lines 9-17 — The poet says the <u>room</u> she was in was clean, empty and <u>soulless</u> (9-11), until she "coloured" it with her <u>shouts and screams</u> during the birth. She says she and her daughter were both desperate to be <u>separate</u> from each other.

Lines 18-29 — The poet says that they're <u>still in a struggle</u> with each other (18-20). She describes a more recent incident when her daughter, now a child, <u>confronts her</u> by asking if she can carry on skating. This makes the poet feel a similar sense of <u>conflict</u> to when her daughter was born.

Learn About the Three Types of Language

1) <u>CONFRONTATIONAL LANGUAGE</u> — Both mother and daughter are desperate to <u>break free</u> from each other. The birth is described as a <u>violent struggle</u> to break apart, and they're still in <u>conflict</u> years later.

2) <u>LOVING LANGUAGE</u> — There are signs of the poet's <u>love</u> for her daughter. These feelings of affection show they have an intense, <u>natural bond</u>.

3) <u>METAPHORICAL LANGUAGE</u> — <u>Rope</u> seems to mean the umbilical cord — but it's also used as a symbol of <u>love</u> and of the <u>power struggle</u> between mother and daughter.

Remember the Feelings and Attitudes in the Poem

AAAAAAAARRRRRRGGGHHHH!!!

1) <u>CONFLICT</u> — The poet feels <u>aggression</u> between her and her daughter.
2) <u>LOVE</u> — She also feels <u>affection</u> and motherly <u>love</u>.
3) <u>CONFUSION</u> — She shows that these <u>mixed feelings</u> have <u>always</u> been there — and maybe they always will.

> The poet's feelings for her daughter are confused. She's torn between hostility and love.

Think About Your Feelings and Attitudes to the Poem

1) Pick 2 words or phrases that <u>stand out to you</u>. If none stand out, just pick 2 <u>unusual words or phrases</u>.
2) Write these 2 words or phrases down. Then write about how they <u>make you feel</u>. If they don't make you feel anything, don't worry — just <u>make something up</u>, as long as it's not too stupid.

> **EXAMPLE** The phrase "the tight / Red rope of love" makes me feel sympathy for the narrator. She seems very confused by her feelings, as the love she feels for her daughter seems to strangle and hurt her. It is hard to see how they will resolve their conflict.

Themes — parent/child relationship, love, strong emotions...

Compare 'Catrin' with other poems about the same themes: <u>parent/child relationships</u> ('Digging' p.44-45 and 'Follower' p.50-51), <u>love</u> ('On my first Sonne' p.6-7 and 'Sonnet 130' p.20-21) and <u>strong emotions</u> ('Mid-Term Break' p.46-47 and 'The Affliction of Margaret' p.10-11).

Baby-sitting

Baby-sitting

There's an unnatural feel to the whole situation for her.

Very straightforward tone seems uncaring.

The baby is snug and happy while she's asleep.

Unemotional, uncaring way of describing a baby.

Short sentences — she sounds calm and certain.

She can only think of the worst things about babies.

Sarcastically describes the baby's smell.

I am sitting in a strange room listening
For the wrong baby. I don't love
This baby. She is sleeping a snuffly
Roseate, bubbling sleep; she is fair;
5   She is a perfectly acceptable child.
I am afraid of her. If she wakes
She will hate me. She will shout
Her hot midnight rage, her nose
Will stream disgustingly and the perfume
10 Of her breath will fail to enchant me.

To her I will represent absolute
Abandonment. For her it will be worse
Than for the lover cold in lonely
Sheets; worse than for the woman who waits
15 A moment to collect her dignity
Beside the bleached bone in the terminal ward.
As she rises sobbing from the monstrous land
Stretching for milk-familiar comforting,
She will find me and between us two
20 It will not come. It will not come.

Another image of betrayed love.

The baby's need for her mother's milk seems natural and right.

Says an abandoned baby feels even worse than people do when someone close to them dies.

She thinks the baby has been having nightmares.

Repetition shows she's certain that she can't comfort the baby.

The baby will want its mother, and the poet won't be able to comfort it.

POEM DICTIONARY
roseate — happy, rose-coloured

Baby-sitting

The poet writes about her feelings when <u>baby-sitting</u> someone else's child. She doesn't love the baby she's looking after because it's <u>not hers</u>. She's worried that when the baby wakes up, she won't be able to give her the <u>comfort</u> she needs, because her mother isn't there. So sad...

You've Got To Know What Happens in the Poem

Lines 1-5 The poet says she's looking after someone else's baby in a house which isn't hers. The baby is sleeping.

Lines 6-10 She's scared that when the baby <u>wakes up</u>, she'll be all noisy, snotty and <u>disgusting</u>.

Lines 11-16 The poet says that when the baby sees her, she'll feel horribly <u>abandoned</u> because <u>her mum isn't there</u>.

Lines 17-20 She says that the baby will want her <u>mother's milk</u> — but she <u>won't get it</u>.

Learn About the Three Types of Language

1) <u>DRY TONE</u> — At times she sounds emotionless. She feels <u>detached</u> (separated) from the baby, and seems to see it as an <u>object</u>, rather than a person.

2) <u>BLEAK LANGUAGE</u> — The poet has a very <u>pessimistic</u> outlook — she predicts nothing but the worst, e.g. that the baby will feel abandoned when she wakes up. The poet sees <u>no way</u> of avoiding this.

3) <u>IMAGERY</u> — There are some pretty <u>depressing</u> images — the poet uses them to describe how awful she thinks the baby will feel when it wakes up and finds its mum isn't there.

Remember the Feelings and Attitudes in the Poem

"Are you old enough to be looking after me?"

1) <u>DISCOMFORT</u> — She feels really <u>uncomfortable</u>, in the "strange room" with the "wrong baby".

2) <u>FEAR</u> — She's <u>scared</u> that she won't be able to give the baby what it needs.

3) <u>SORROW</u> — She feels <u>despair</u> at the "Abandonment" of the baby.

She completely focuses on the negatives of baby-sitting — ignoring the more positive aspects, like getting paid for basically watching TV and texting your mates.

Think About Your Feelings and Attitudes to the Poem

1) Pick 2 words or phrases that <u>stand out to you</u>. If none stand out, just pick 2 <u>unusual words or phrases</u>.

2) Write these 2 words or phrases down. Then write about how they <u>make you feel</u>. If they don't make you feel anything, don't worry — just <u>make something up</u>, as long as it's not too stupid.

EXAMPLE I find the phrase "I don't love / This baby" shocking. The baby-sitter does not seem to feel any emotions at all for the baby, but I would expect anyone looking after a baby to feel at least something for it.

Themes — imagery, first person and strong emotions...

Compare 'Baby-sitting' with other poems about similar themes: <u>imagery</u> ('At a Potato Digging' p.36-37 and 'On the Train' p.64-65), use of the <u>first person</u> ('Follower' p.50-51 and 'On my first Sonne' p.6-7) and <u>strong emotions</u> ('Mid-Term Break' p.46-47 and 'Catrin' p.52-53).

Mali

Mali

The poet feels like she did when her daughter was born. She didn't think she'd have this kind of feeling again.

Three years ago to the hour, the day she was born,
that unmistakable brim and tug of the tide
I'd thought was over. I drove
the twenty miles of summer lanes,
5   my daughter cursing Sunday cars,
and the lazy swish of a dairy herd
rocking so slowly home.

The birth is part of a natural cycle — like the tides going in and out.

The apples are ripe and ready to be picked — just like the baby is ready to be born.

Bright natural colours.

Read these 2 lines together — the lines in the middle describe the scene.

Something in the event,
late summer heat overspilling into harvest,
10   apples reddening on heavy trees,
the lanes sweet with brambles
and our fingers purple,
then the child coming easy,
too soon, in the wrong place,

She's born early, before they can get to hospital.

The premature birth is like a plant growing in the wrong season.

15   things seasonal and out of season
towed home a harvest moon.
My daughter's daughter
a day old under an umbrella on the beach
late-comer at summer's festival,
20   and I'm hooked again, life-sentenced.
Even the sea could not draw me from her.

She has no choice in loving her granddaughter.

Sounds like nature is throwing a party.

Their natural bond is stronger than the tides mentioned in line 2.

This year I bake her a cake like our house,
and old trees blossom
with balloons and streamers.
25   We celebrate her with a cup
of cold blue ocean,
candles at twilight, and three drops of,
probably, last blood.

Colourful decorations to celebrate Mali's birthday.

They celebrate everything about Mali, not just the fact that it's her birthday.

One for each year of her life.

This probably means "blood" as in kinship ties. The poet thinks this will be the last time she sees a new addition to her family.

POEM DICTIONARY
harvest moon — a full moon in autumn
twilight — fading light after sunset

Mali

This poem is about the birth of the poet's <u>granddaughter</u>, called Mali. The poet compares the birth to the summer <u>harvest</u>, and describes how she felt an intense love for Mali like she did when her own daughter was born.

You've Got To Know *What Happens in the Poem*

<u>Lines 1-7</u>	On her granddaughter Mali's <u>third birthday</u>, the poet remembers driving her daughter to hospital to <u>give birth</u> to Mali. But they get <u>held up</u> on a country lane.
<u>Lines 8-14</u>	The poet remembers the scene. It's summer, with the <u>harvest</u> beginning and lots of colour all around. The baby was born quickly, before they arrived at hospital.
<u>Lines 15-21</u>	When Mali was just a day old, the poet felt an incredibly <u>strong bond</u> with her.
<u>Lines 22-28</u>	The family <u>celebrate</u> at Mali's third birthday party. The poet says Mali will probably be the <u>last new addition</u> to the family in the poet's lifetime.

Learn About the *Three Types of Language*

1) <u>NEW LIFE</u> — The events are <u>familiar</u> to the poet — they remind her of when she gave birth to her daughter. The birth of her granddaughter is the start of a <u>new phase</u> in the <u>life cycle</u> of the family.

2) <u>NATURAL LANGUAGE</u> — The birth is linked to the natural cycles of the <u>moon</u> and the <u>tides</u>. The ripe fruit of the <u>harvest</u> is compared to the baby.

3) <u>LANGUAGE OF CELEBRATION</u> — There's <u>joy</u> at the birth of the child, and it seems as if <u>nature</u> is part of the celebration. At the end of the poem they celebrate her third <u>birthday</u>.

Remember the *Feelings and Attitudes in the Poem*

1) <u>JOY</u> — She's <u>happy</u> at the birth of her granddaughter, and she <u>loves</u> her.

2) <u>APPREHENSION</u> — But she's also <u>nervous</u> about her — she thinks there'll be bad times as well as good (line 20).

3) <u>CONNECTION</u> — She feels a strong <u>connection with nature</u>, because of the birth and her memories of giving birth herself.

Think About *Your Feelings and Attitudes to the Poem*

1) Pick 2 words or phrases that <u>stand out to you</u>. If none stand out, just pick 2 <u>unusual words or phrases</u>.

2) Write these 2 words or phrases down. Then write about how they <u>make you feel</u>. If they don't make you feel anything, don't worry — just <u>make something up</u>, as long as it's not too stupid.

> **EXAMPLE** When the poet says "Even the sea could not draw me from her", I really admire her. It seems that she will always be there for her granddaughter, which I think is really brave, as she knows it will not be easy.

Themes — *nature, memory and imagery...*

Compare 'Mali' with other poems about the same themes: <u>nature</u> ('Blackberry-Picking' p.40-41 and 'Sonnet' p.34-35), <u>memory</u> ('Perch' p.38-39 and 'Digging' p.44-45) and <u>imagery</u> ('Death of a Naturalist' p.42-43 and 'The Field-Mouse' p.60-61).

Section Three — Gillian Clarke

A Difficult Birth, Easter 1998

The Good Friday Agreement was a famous peace agreement in Northern Ireland. In Christianity, Good Friday is the date of Christ's death, before his resurrection.

They'd given up hope of the ewe having lambs — just as some had given up hope of peace in Northern Ireland.

A Difficult Birth, Easter 1998

An old ewe that somehow till this year
had given the ram the slip. We thought her barren.
Good Friday, and the Irish peace deal close,
and tonight she's serious, restless and hoofing the straw.
5 We put off the quiet supper and bottle of wine
we'd planned, to celebrate if the news is good.

Like the Last Supper — Jesus' last meal with his disciples.

A sign that she's ready to give birth.

This is when the troubles in Northern Ireland first broke out.

Her waters broke an hour ago and she's sipped
her own lost salty ocean from the ground.
While they slog it out in Belfast, eight decades
10 since Easter 1916, exhausted, tamed by pain,
she licks my fingers with a burning tongue,
lies down again. Two hooves and a muzzle.

The lamb is stuck, like the peace talks in Northern Ireland.

Looking for a sign of hope.

Doctors helping women experiencing difficult births.

But the lamb won't come. You phone for help
and step into the lane to watch for car lights.
15 This is when the whitecoats come to the women,
well-meaning, knowing best, with their needles and forceps.
So I ease my fingers in, take the slippery head
in my right hand, two hooves in my left.

The poet and the ewe struggle together for a common goal — like the different sides in the Irish peace process.

The lamb is small and vulnerable — it's a fragile peace.

We strain together, harder than we dared.
20 I feel a creak in the limbs and pull till he comes
in a syrupy flood. She drinks him, famished, and you find us
peaceful, at a cradling that might have been a death.
Then the second lamb slips through her opened door,
the stone rolled away.

Christians believe that when the stone at the entrance to Christ's tomb was rolled away, it was a sign of his resurrection.

Both the physical chance for the second lamb to be born, and the chance for peace.

POEM DICTIONARY
ewe — female sheep
ram — male sheep
barren — unable to have children
Good Friday — in Christianity, this is the day of Christ's death, before his resurrection on Easter Sunday.
Irish peace deal — The Good Friday Agreement set out a plan for government of Northern Ireland elected
      by the people of Northern Ireland
Belfast — capital of Northern Ireland, where there have been violent troubles between Catholics and Protestants since 1916
forceps — tool used to help deliver babies

A Difficult Birth, Easter 1998

This poem describes an <u>old sheep giving birth</u>. It's a struggle against the odds, but in the end the lambs are born safely. This is used as a metaphor for the struggle for <u>peace in Northern Ireland</u>.

You've Got To Know What Happens in the Poem

<u>Lines 1-6</u>　　An old sheep is in pain — she's about to <u>give birth</u> to her first lambs.

<u>Lines 7-12</u>　　The poet describes the <u>peace talks</u> in Belfast, and the ewe's difficulties in giving birth.

<u>Lines 13-18</u>　　They call for <u>help</u>, but none arrives. The poet thinks of when people try to help women give birth. She reaches in to try to <u>pull the lamb out</u>.

<u>Lines 19-24</u>　　After a struggle, the lamb is <u>born safely</u>. Then <u>another one</u> arrives — bonus.

Learn About the Three Types of Language

1) <u>WAR and PEACE</u> — The birth of the lambs stands for the <u>birth of peace</u> in Northern Ireland. The poet refers to the <u>peace talks</u> in Belfast, which are going on at the time of the birth.

2) <u>RELIGIOUS REFERENCES</u> — Easter is significant for Christians — it's the time when Christ died and was <u>resurrected</u> (born again). In the poem, this <u>religious symbol of new life</u> is linked to the <u>unexpected birth</u> of the lambs and also <u>peace</u> after all the troubles. It's also relevant because the <u>troubles</u> in Northern Ireland were based around religion (conflict between Catholics and Protestants).

3) <u>METAPHORICAL LANGUAGE</u> — The details of the birth are a metaphor for the <u>difficulties</u> and eventual <u>breakthrough</u> in the Good Friday Agreement in Belfast.

Remember the Feelings and Attitudes in the Poem

Sheep — bringers of wool and peace.

1) <u>WORRY</u> — She's <u>worried</u> about the sheep and lamb, and about the situation in Northern Ireland.

2) <u>RELIEF</u> — She's <u>relieved</u> and <u>happy</u> when the birth and the peace talks turn out all right.

Think About Your Feelings and Attitudes to the Poem

1) Pick 2 words or phrases that <u>stand out to you</u>. If none stand out, just pick 2 <u>unusual words or phrases</u>.

2) Write these 2 words or phrases down. Then write about how they <u>make you feel</u>. If they don't make you feel anything, don't worry — just <u>make something up</u>, as long as it's not too stupid.

> **EXAMPLE** When I first read the line, "We strain together, harder than we dared", I felt very nervous. The poet and the ewe are pulling together to try to bring about a happy outcome. It brings home to me just how tense the peace talks must have been.

Themes — politics, nature and imagery...

Compare 'A Difficult Birth, Easter 1998' with other poems about the same themes: <u>politics</u> ('At a Potato Digging' p.36-37 and 'The Field-Mouse' p.60-61), <u>nature</u> ('Storm on the Island' p.48-49 and 'Perch' p.38-39) and <u>imagery</u> ('Digging' p.44-45 and 'Tichborne's Elegy' p.14-15).

The Field-Mouse

The Field-Mouse

The scene appears peaceful at the start of the poem.

Makes the harvest sound violent — linking it to the bombs.

Their neighbour is peaceful and pleasant.

The child wants to protect the mouse.

Pain takes over its whole body.

Summer, and the long grass is a snare drum.
The air hums with jets.
Down at the end of the meadow,
far from the radio's terrible news,
5 we cut the hay. All afternoon
its wave breaks before the tractor blade.
Over the hedge our neighbour travels his field
in a cloud of lime, drifting our land
with a chance gift of sweetness.

10 The child comes running through the killed flowers,
his hands a nest of quivering mouse,
its black eyes two sparks burning.
We know it will die and ought to finish it off.
It curls in agony big as itself
15 and the star goes out in its eye.
Summer in Europe, the field's hurt,
and the children kneel in long grass,
staring at what we have crushed.

Before day's done the field lies bleeding,
20 the dusk garden inhabited by the saved, voles,
frogs, a nest of mice. The wrong that woke
from a rumour of pain won't heal,
and we can't face the newspapers.
All night I dream the children dance in grass
25 their bones brittle as mouse-ribs, the air
stammering with gunfire, my neighbour turned
stranger, wounding my land with stones.

Here the jets are harmless, but in Europe they bring bombs and destruction.

They feel completely separate from the war at this stage.

Sign of the harvest's destruction.

The last signs of life fade away.

The field is personified — the harvest has killed it.

They can't face finding out about the full horror of the war.

Her children are as weak and vulnerable as the mouse in the field.

Onomatopoeia is used to describe the repeated firing sounds of the guns.

In her dream, her neighbour has turned into her enemy — just as neighbours in former-Yugoslavia have done.

POEM DICTIONARY
lime — a substance used to make fields better for growing crops

The Field-Mouse

Key Poem

This poem is set at harvest time on a farm. It's the early 90s, and <u>war</u> is going on abroad in <u>former-Yugoslavia</u>. The poet's family are cutting hay on the farm, when a <u>mouse</u> which has been hurt in the harvest makes the poet think of the <u>innocent victims</u> of the war abroad.

You've Got To Know *What Happens in the Poem*

<u>Lines 1-6</u>	The poet and other people are <u>cutting the hay</u> in their field.
<u>Lines 7-9</u>	The owner of the field next door adds <u>lime</u> to his field, sending a <u>sweet smell</u> over the hedge.
<u>Lines 10-18</u>	A child runs over with a <u>dying mouse</u>, which has been hurt in the hay-cutting. This is compared to <u>children</u> being <u>killed by bombs</u> in former-Yugoslavia.
<u>Lines 19-23</u>	At the end of the day, they've finished cutting the hay. They've heard about what's happened in former-Yugoslavia, but <u>can't face</u> reading about the details.
<u>Lines 24-27</u>	The poet has a <u>nightmare</u> about her neighbour attacking her land and children.

Learn About the *Three Types of Language*

1) <u>IDEALISTIC LANGUAGE</u> — The harvesters' life seems <u>peaceful</u>. At first they feel like they're <u>separate</u> from events elsewhere — until the poet starts making <u>connections</u> between the harvest and the war.

2) <u>VIOLENT LANGUAGE</u> — The chopping down of the <u>hay</u> comes to stand for the war in <u>former-Yugoslavia</u>. The <u>brutality</u> and <u>cruelty</u> of the war is shocking.

3) <u>METAPHORICAL LANGUAGE</u> — The <u>mouse's death</u> from the harvest is a metaphor for the <u>innocent children</u> dying in the war.

Remember the *Feelings and Attitudes in the Poem*

1) <u>CONCERN</u> — The poet is <u>worried</u> about the children in former-Yugoslavia.
2) <u>GUILT</u> — She feels <u>guilty</u> and responsible for what's happening (line 18).
3) <u>FEAR</u> — She's <u>scared</u> of just how bad the situation there might be (line 23).

> In her nightmare, she's <u>scared</u> that her <u>own children</u> will suffer in the same way as the children in former-Yugoslavia.

Think About *Your Feelings and Attitudes to the Poem*

1) Pick 2 words or phrases that <u>stand out to you</u>. If none stand out, just pick 2 <u>unusual words or phrases</u>.
2) Write these 2 words or phrases down. Then write about how they <u>make you feel</u>. If they don't make you feel anything, don't worry — just <u>make something up</u>, as long as it's not too stupid.

> **EXAMPLE** The description of the poet's children as having "bones brittle as mouse-ribs" makes me realise how helpless the victims of war are. I find this really scary and shocking as, even though this is a dream, the poet shows that this situation could happen anywhere.

Themes — *politics, danger and imagery...*

Compare 'The Field-Mouse' with other poems about the same themes: <u>politics</u> ('At a Potato Digging' p.36-37 and 'A Difficult Birth, Easter 1998' p.58-59), <u>danger</u> ('Storm on the Island' p.48-49 and 'Patrolling Barnegat' p.18-19) and <u>imagery</u> ('Blackberry-Picking' p.40-41 and 'Sonnet' p.34-35).

62

October

October

We know from the title that the poem is set in autumn.

The broken branch is personified like it's part of a dead person.

The trees sound old and frail as they take on their autumn colours.

Bluntly tells us what's happening.

The weather is linked to the sadness of the people at the funeral.

Simile.

The theme of death is introduced.

Alliteration emphasises the sound of the rain.

The overgrown plants look like tangled hair.

Going back to nature.

The sound of the earth hitting the coffin is shocking.

There's an urgent, hurried feel to this stanza.

More reminders of autumn.

She wants to achieve as much as possible before she dies.

Wind in the poplars and a broken branch,
a dead arm in the bright trees. Five poplars
tremble gradually to gold. The stone face
of the lion darkens in a sharp shower,
5 his dreadlocks of lobelia grown long,
tangled, more brown now than blue-eyed.

My friend dead and the graveyard at Orcop —
her short ride to the hawthorn hedge, lighter
than hare-bones on men's shoulders, our faces
10 stony, rain, weeping in the air. The grave
deep as a well takes the earth's thud, the slow
fall of flowers.

              Over the page the pen
runs faster than wind's white steps over grass.
For a while health feels like pain. Then panic
15 running the fields, the grass, the racing leaves
ahead of light, holding that robin's eye
in the laurel, hydrangeas' faded green.
I must write like the wind, year after year
passing my death-day, winning ground.

POEM DICTIONARY
poplars — a type of tall tree
dreadlocks — matted locks of hair
lobelia — a type of plant with coloured flowers
Orcop — an English village close to the Welsh border
laurel — the name of a type of small evergreen tree
hydrangea — a type of tree with coloured flowers

Section Three — Gillian Clarke

October

This poem is about the <u>funeral</u> of one of the poet's friends. There are lots of images of <u>autumn</u>, which make the poet think about death — she's in the autumn years of her life. The poet thinks she may not be alive for all that much longer, so has to <u>make the most</u> of what life she has left.

You've Got To Know What Happens in the Poem

Lines 1-6	The poet describes an <u>autumnal scene</u>, with bare, broken <u>trees</u> and an overgrown sculpture.
Lines 7-12	She's at the <u>funeral</u> of a <u>friend</u>. It rains as her friend is <u>buried</u>.
Lines 12-19	The poet realises that <u>she'll die too</u>, and has to write as much as she can before she dies.

Learn About the Three Types of Language

1) <u>LANGUAGE ABOUT DEATH</u> — As well as the fact that there's a <u>funeral</u> going on, the theme of <u>death</u> is suggested by the dead branch of a tree and <u>faded colours</u>.

2) <u>AUTUMNAL LANGUAGE</u> — The bad weather and autumnal colours emphasise the idea of <u>death</u> at the funeral. Images of autumn also remind the poet that she is in the <u>autumn years</u> of her life.

3) <u>NATURE</u> — The poet describes nature in detail — using it to represent both <u>death</u> and her <u>need to go on living</u> (line 18).

Remember the Feelings and Attitudes in the Poem

1) <u>SADNESS</u> — The poet is <u>sad</u> about the death of her friend.
2) <u>FEAR</u> — She's <u>worried</u> that she doesn't have long left to live herself.
3) <u>DETERMINATION</u> — She's <u>determined</u> to do as much as possible with the time she has left.

Think About Your Feelings and Attitudes to the Poem

1) Pick 2 words or phrases that <u>stand out to you</u>. If none stand out, just pick 2 <u>unusual words or phrases</u>.
2) Write these 2 words or phrases down. Then write about how they <u>make you feel</u>. If they don't make you feel anything, don't worry — just <u>make something up</u>, as long as it's not too stupid.

> **EXAMPLE** The description of "rain, weeping in the air" makes me feel sad. It feels like the whole world, even the weather, is mourning for the loss of the poet's friend. It also makes it seem that death is always around us, wherever we are.

Themes — death, nature and imagery...

Compare 'October' with other poems about the same themes: <u>death</u> ('Mid-Term Break' p.46-47 and 'On my first Sonne' p.6-7), <u>nature</u> ('Perch' p.38-39 and 'Inversnaid' p.32-33), and <u>imagery</u> ('At a Potato Digging' p.36-37 and 'Mali' p.56-57).

On the Train

On the Train

The train the poet is on protects its passengers like they're children.

Cradled through England between flooded fields
rocking, rocking the rails, my head-phones on,
the black box of my Walkman on the table.
Hot tea trembles in its plastic cup.
5 I'm thinking of you waking in our bed
thinking of me on the train. Too soon to phone.

The radio speaks in the suburbs, in commuter towns,
in cars unloading children at school gates,
is silenced in dark parkways down the line
10 before locks click and footprints track the frost
and trains slide out of stations in the dawn
dreaming their way towards the blazing bone-ship.

The Vodafone you are calling
may have been switched off.
15 Please call later. And calling later,
calling later their phones ring in the rubble
and in the rubble of suburban kitchens
the wolves howl into silent telephones.

I phone. No answer. Where are you now?
20 The train moves homeward through the morning.
Tonight I'll be home safe, but talk to me, please.
Pick up the phone. Today I'm tolerant
of mobiles. Let them say it. I'll say it too.
Darling, I'm on the train.

Alliteration and rhythm create an impression of the sound of the train.

Suggests the fear that others will be feeling.

She wants to phone, but feels she should wait.

News of the crash spreads quickly.

A recorded message as they can't get through to loved ones — a bad sign.

Horrible image — like a shipwreck. Contrasts with the sleepy quietness of the lines that come before.

Meaning changes from the rubble of the crash to the rubble of people's lives, wrecked by what's happened.

Animal-like cry of distress when there's no response.

Short sentences make her sound anxious.

She's desperate to get in touch.

Usually an empty statement, but now has an important meaning — she's safe.

POEM DICTIONARY
suburbs — areas on the outskirts of a town or city
commuter towns — towns where people live but travel to work somewhere else every day

On the Train

The poet is travelling by train on the day of the <u>Paddington train crash</u> in 1999. She tries to phone her husband so that he doesn't worry about her, but she <u>can't get through</u> to him. She thinks of all the people who'll be anxiously phoning up <u>loved ones</u> to find out if they're ok.

You've Got To Know What Happens in the Poem

<u>Lines 1-6</u>	The poet is travelling on a <u>train</u>. She thinks of her husband waking up, <u>wondering if she's ok</u>.
<u>Lines 7-12</u>	She describes the <u>news of the crash</u> reaching people across the country.
<u>Lines 13-18</u>	<u>Friends and relatives</u> of people who might be on the train which has crashed try to phone them — but <u>can't get through</u>.
<u>Lines 19-24</u>	The poet tries to phone her husband to say she's all right, but she <u>can't get through either</u>.

Learn About the Three Types of Language

1) <u>FEARFUL LANGUAGE</u> — The poet imagines the <u>fear</u> people must be going through as they try to phone their loved ones. When phones <u>aren't answered</u>, it seems to be a <u>terrible sign</u>.

2) <u>REFERENCES TO TECHNOLOGY</u> — <u>Mobile phones</u> are an important theme — the poet imagines people using them to try and find out their loved ones are ok. For once mobiles have a <u>serious use</u> — phrases which are usually just <u>annoying</u>, like "I'm on the train", become <u>important</u> and <u>meaningful</u>.

3) <u>METAPHORICAL LANGUAGE</u> — <u>Trains</u> are described as if they're <u>protective</u> and <u>comforting</u> at the start of the poem, but <u>deadly</u> later on. The desperate cries of relatives are described as the howls of <u>wolves</u>.

Remember the Feelings and Attitudes in the Poem

1) <u>ANXIETY</u> — The poet is <u>worried</u> that her husband will think she's been hurt in the crash.

2) <u>DESPERATION</u> — She's <u>desperate</u> to get in touch with him.

3) <u>EMPATHY</u> — She <u>feels sorry</u> for all the people who are worrying about loved ones.

> The poet is anxious to let her husband know she's all right, but thinks of those who won't receive such good news.

Think About Your Feelings and Attitudes to the Poem

1) Pick 2 words or phrases that <u>stand out to you</u>. If none stand out, just pick 2 <u>unusual words or phrases</u>.

2) Write these 2 words or phrases down. Then write about how they <u>make you feel</u>. If they don't make you feel anything, don't worry — just <u>make something up</u>, as long as it's not too stupid.

> **EXAMPLE** I find the line "the wolves howl into silent telephones" shocking and horrifying. It creates a terrible image of how devastated the relatives of the victims of the crash are feeling. They are unable to do anything but scream in terror, like wild animals.

Themes — death, first person, language effects...

Compare 'On the Train' with other poems about the same themes: <u>death</u> ('Mid-Term Break' p.46-47 and 'October' p.62-63), <u>use of first person</u> ('Baby-sitting' p.54-55 and 'The Man He Killed' p.16-17) and <u>language effects</u> ('Perch' p.38-39 and 'At a Potato Digging' p.36-37).

Cold Knap Lake

Cold Knap Lake

Sounds like she's dead at this point.

We once watched a crowd
pull a drowned child from the lake.
Blue-lipped and dressed in water's long green silk
she lay for dead.

She's covered in pond weeds. The "silk" contrasts with her "poor house" (line 13).

Dramatic descriptions of her mother's bravery.

5   Then kneeling on the earth,
a heroine, her red head bowed,
her wartime cotton frock soaked,
my mother gave a stranger's child her breath.
The crowd stood silent,
10   drawn by the dread of it.

It's as if the poet's mother has performed a miracle — bringing the child back to life.

Alliteration adds to the drama of the story.

The child breathed, bleating
and rosy in my mother's hands.
My father took her home to a poor house
and watched her thrashed for almost drowning.

A shocking image, but the poet sounds unemotional.

Short line makes it sound like she's stopped to think about it.

15   Was I there?
Or is that troubled surface something else
shadowy under the dipped fingers of willows
where satiny mud blooms in cloudiness
after the treading, heavy webs of swans
20   as their wings beat and whistle on the air?

The surface of the lake — but also her uncertain memory.

What she saw was dark and unclear — her imagination might have made up the memory.

The water was muddy and unclear, like the memory.

These lines sum up her thoughts — she thinks memories are mysterious.

All lost things lie under closing water
in that lake with the poor man's daughter.

Rhyming couplet brings the poem to a neat conclusion.

POEM DICTIONARY
willows — a type of tree with long, thin branches
satiny — smooth, glossy (like satin)

Cold Knap Lake

The poet describes a time when her mother <u>rescued a drowning girl</u> from a lake.
Then she wonders whether the memory is <u>real</u> or not. Place your bets...

You've Got To Know What Happens in the Poem

<u>Lines 1-4</u>   The poet remembers seeing a crowd gathered around a <u>girl</u> who's just been <u>pulled out of a lake</u>.
<u>Lines 5-12</u>   She describes how <u>her mother saved the girl</u> by giving her mouth-to-mouth resuscitation.
<u>Lines 13-14</u> The poet's father took the girl home, where she was <u>beaten</u> by her own father.
<u>Lines 15-22</u> The poet wonders whether the memory is <u>real</u> — it could have been <u>something else</u> in the muddy lake. She says memories often become <u>confused</u>.

Learn About the Two Types of Language

1) <u>DRAMATIC LANGUAGE</u> — The poet's descriptions of how her mother revived the girl make the story sound almost <u>too amazing to be true</u>. This is maybe why the poet wonders if she's <u>imagined it</u>.

2) <u>PHILOSOPHICAL LANGUAGE</u> — The poet <u>questions herself</u> and <u>wonders</u> about how memories work. The <u>uncertain</u> language in the last two verses adds to the idea that things <u>might not have actually happened</u> as she remembers them. She tries to come up with some <u>answers</u> to tie things together.

Remember the Feelings and Attitudes in the Poem

Real or imaginary?

1) <u>ADMIRATION</u> — The poet <u>admires</u> her mother for saving the girl.
2) <u>CONFUSION</u> — She's <u>confused</u> about what's real and what's imagined.
3) <u>WONDER</u> — She's fairly <u>philosophical</u> at the end of the poem — she says that memories can get blurred, and that's just how it is.

> The feel of the poem changes sharply at line 15 — it starts off with dramatic, vivid images, then changes to an uncertain, wondering tone.

Think About Your Feelings and Attitudes to the Poem

1) Pick 2 words or phrases that <u>stand out to you</u>. If none stand out, just pick 2 <u>unusual words or phrases</u>.
2) Write these 2 words or phrases down. Then write about how they <u>make you feel</u>. If they don't make you feel anything, don't worry — just <u>make something up</u>, as long as it's not too stupid.

> **EXAMPLE** I find the phrase "satiny mud blooms in cloudiness" really interesting.
> It is a very clever way of describing how memories can become muddled and unclear.

Themes — memory, danger, closing couplet...

Compare 'Cold Knap Lake' with other poems about the same themes: <u>memory</u> ('Digging' p.44-45 and 'Catrin' p.52-53), <u>danger</u> ('Storm on the Island' p.48-49 and 'The Field-Mouse' p.60-61) and use of a <u>closing couplet</u> ('Sonnet 130' p.20-21 and 'The Village Schoolmaster' p.28-29).

Nature

Loads of poets write about nature. Sometimes it's just because they like the countryside. Other times it's because they see nature as a metaphor for all the other stuff going on in their life.

> 1) The <u>beauty and power</u> of nature can be exciting.
> 2) Nature can also be <u>cruel and destructive</u> — a threat to human life.
> 3) Nature needs to be treated with <u>respect</u> and not taken for granted.

Some Poets Celebrate *Nature's Beauty*

Inversnaid (Pages 32-33)

1) The poet <u>loves</u> the scene he describes. He feels <u>protective</u> of it — "Long live the weeds and the wilderness yet".
2) He <u>finds beauty</u> in a scene which is pretty <u>bleak and wild</u> — the muddy river is described as a "darksome burn, horseback brown", and the foam on the water as a "windpuff-bonnet".

Sonnet (Pages 34-35)

1) The poet describes the <u>countryside in summer</u>.
2) He describes the <u>colours</u> of nature — the "white wool sack clouds" and the "Mare blobs stain with gold the meadow drain". This helps the reader imagine the <u>beauty</u> of the scene.
3) He describes the <u>wildlife</u> in the scene with a lot of <u>affection</u>: "the Moor Hen", the "bright beetles" and the "insects happy wings". This shows that he's <u>observed the scene</u> in detail: he really cares about it.

Some Poets write about the *Power of Nature*

Mali (Pages 56-57)

1) In this poem, Clarke <u>links</u> the <u>birth</u> of her granddaughter with <u>nature</u>.
2) Her granddaughter's birth reminds her of her daughter's birth — it's a <u>cycle of new life</u>.
3) She describes the birth as like the "unmistakable brim and tug of the tide". It's part of an <u>old, familiar pattern</u>, as <u>regular</u> as the tide going in and out.
4) Her <u>love</u> for her new granddaughter is <u>compared</u> to the <u>strength of nature</u>: "Even the sea could not draw me from her".

Storm on the Island (Pages 48-49)

1) The poet uses the language of <u>war</u> to stress the sheer <u>strength of the storm</u>, e.g. "Exploding", "strafes" and "bombarded".
2) He shows how the <u>people</u> who live on the island are <u>vulnerable</u> and at the mercy of the storm. There is "no natural shelter".
3) The poet says you should respect the <u>power of nature</u>. It can be "like a tame cat / Turned savage" — turning on you when you least expect it.

She may look cute, but she'll get you.

The Eagle (Pages 24-25)

1) The poet creates a picture of a very <u>powerful creature</u> — "like a thunderbolt he falls".
2) He shows the eagle is <u>dominant</u> over his surroundings — "The wrinkled sea beneath him crawls".

Look out the window...

Clarke and Heaney both describe nature in several of their poems, often using it as a <u>metaphor</u>. Some other poems about nature are: 'Patrolling Barnegat' (p.18-19), 'At a Potato Digging' (p.36-37), 'Perch' (p.38-39), 'Digging' (p.44-45), 'The Field-Mouse' (p.60-61) and 'October' (p.62-63).

Death

Death is something people feel <u>emotional</u> about — so it's a good theme for poetry.

> 1) The death of a loved one causes <u>grief</u> and a sense of <u>loss</u>.
> 2) Everyone dies — it's something we need to <u>prepare</u> for.
> 3) Deaths caused by <u>war, crime or execution</u> can seem an unnecessary waste of life.
> 4) Sometimes people <u>kill</u> out of <u>anger</u> or desire for <u>revenge</u>.

Some Poets write about Killing and Murder

The Man He Killed (Pages 16-17)

Maybe we should just go for a pint.

1) In this poem, a soldier talks about a man he <u>killed during a battle</u>. He points out the <u>irony</u> that if he had met the man in other circumstances, they might have been friends.
2) He imagines that the man he killed was rather <u>like himself</u>. He might have only joined the army because he was <u>unemployed</u> and needed a job. Even though officially the man was his "<u>foe</u>", there wasn't necessarily anything bad about him.
3) The poem points out how <u>foolish and wasteful</u> the <u>killing in war</u> is: "You shoot a fellow down / You'd treat if met where any bar is".

The Laboratory (Pages 30-31)

1) The woman in this poem wants to <u>kill her lover's new mistress</u>.
2) She is obsessed by her <u>jealousy</u> and the idea of <u>violent revenge</u>. She sounds <u>excited</u> by the idea of killing and causing <u>pain</u> — "Let death be felt and the proof remain".
3) Getting the poison to kill her rival makes the woman <u>elated and happy</u>. She even offers to kiss the old man who's prepared the poison.

Other Poets write about Grief and Loss

On my first Sonne (Pages 6-7)

1) The poet shows his <u>grief</u> over the <u>loss of a child</u>: "Farewell, thou child of my right hand, and joy".
2) The poet tries to find something <u>positive</u> in his son's death — that at least the boy has escaped many of life's troubles and old age.
3) He pays <u>tribute</u> to his son, by saying he was "his best piece of poetrie" — his best work. He decides <u>never</u> to love anything so much again, in case he <u>loses</u> it.

October (Pages 62-63)

1) The poet describes a <u>friend's funeral</u>, one autumn.
2) The <u>autumn weather</u> is linked to <u>death</u> and grief — the "rain, weeping in the air", the wind causing a "broken branch, / a dead arm in the bright trees".
3) She describes the funeral in quite a <u>brutal</u> way which suggests she <u>feels hurt</u> by it — "My friend dead", "her short ride to the hawthorn hedge", "the earth's thud".
4) Her friend's death makes her <u>think about her own death</u>. It makes her "panic", but it also makes her <u>determined</u> to make the most of the life she's got left.

This topic's a bit bleak...

There are <u>many different attitudes to death</u> in the poems from the Anthology — sadness, acceptance, bitterness... Other poems which talk about death are: 'Tichborne's Elegy' (p.14-15), 'Ulysses' (p.26-27), 'Mid-Term Break' (p.46-47) and 'On the Train' (p.64-65).

Parent/Child Relationships

Family arguments — a valuable source of poetic inspiration.

1) The parent/child relationship is <u>central</u> to most people's lives.
2) Parent/child relationships often <u>change</u> as the people grow older.
3) Parent/child relationships often contain some <u>conflict</u>.

Some Children want Independence from their Parents

Catrin (Pages 52-53)

1) The poet remembers the <u>birth of her daughter</u>. She describes it as "our first / Fierce confrontation". The <u>struggle for independence</u> between mother and daughter had already begun.
2) The poet says that there is a "<u>rope of love</u>" pulling her and her daughter together, but at the same time they have always been struggling to be separate: "To be two, to be ourselves".
3) As her daughter asks if she can "skate / In the dark, for one more hour" the poet feels torn. She understands her daughter's <u>urge to be independent</u>, but at the same time she feels loving and <u>protective</u> of her.

Parents and Children can have very Different Characters

Ulysses (Pages 26-27)

1) The narrator of this poem is the great Greek hero Ulysses. He's <u>old</u> now, but still desperate for travel and adventure. He says, "I cannot rest from travel: I will drink / Life to the lees".
2) He's <u>bored</u> and <u>frustrated</u> with living at home with his "agèd wife", ruling a "savage race" of people.
3) Ulysses describes his son, <u>Telemachus</u>, as having a <u>very different character</u> and outlook to himself. Telemachus is happy to patiently rule the island, and gradually "make mild / A rugged people".
4) When Ulysses describes Telemachus and his work, he uses words and phrases that suggest <u>dullness</u> and <u>caution</u> like "slow prudence", "useful", "duties" and "decent". These are in strong <u>contrast</u> to the <u>vibrant</u> way he describes <u>himself</u>, e.g. "a hungry heart", "honoured" and "yearning in desire".

Digging (Pages 44-45)

1) The poet sees his old father digging in the garden, and this reminds him of <u>how skilled and strong</u> his <u>father and grandfather</u> used to be at <u>digging</u> — "By God, the old man could handle a spade".
2) The poet hasn't followed in their footsteps — he's <u>inside writing</u>, not outside digging. He says, "I've no spade to follow men like them".
3) At the end of the poem, he draws a <u>parallel</u> between <u>digging and writing</u>: "The squat pen rests. / I'll dig with it". He wants to get the same pride and strength from writing as his elders did from digging.

Most Parents Care Deeply about their Children

The Affliction of Margaret (Pages 10-11)

1) The woman in the poem hasn't heard from her son for <u>7 years</u>. We see her <u>despair</u> at not knowing whether her son is <u>dead or alive</u> — "My apprehensions come in crowds".
2) She's <u>desperate</u> to hear from him, whatever has happened to him: "Oh find me, prosperous or undone!".
3) She describes her son as if he's almost <u>perfect</u>: "He was among the prime in worth".
4) She really <u>loves</u> her son, but we <u>don't</u> find out how he feels about her.

Everyone starts off as a screaming baby...

Other poems which describe parent/child relationships are 'On my first Sonne' (p.6-7), 'Mali' (p.56-57), 'The Field-Mouse' (p.60-61) and 'Cold Knap Lake' (p.66-67).

Danger

Some people are <u>scared</u> by danger — others get a <u>kick out of it</u>.

> 1) Danger can arise from the <u>natural environment</u>, e.g. storms.
> 2) Danger can also be <u>caused by people</u> — through aggression and violence.
> 3) Sometimes a <u>danger</u> is just in people's imaginations — it doesn't really exist.

Danger can come from the <u>Environment</u>

<u>Patrolling Barnegat</u> (Pages 18-19)

1) The poem describes a small band of watchmen patrolling the beach during a <u>fierce storm</u>.
2) The storm is described as very <u>powerful</u>: "Waves, air, midnight, their savagest trinity lashing".
   It is an <u>uncontrollable</u> part of nature: "Wild, wild the storm".
3) The storm is <u>dangerous</u> — out to sea the watchmen wonder if they can see a <u>wrecked ship</u>:
   "is that a wreck? is the red signal flaring?".

<u>The Little Boy Lost</u> and <u>The Little Boy Found</u> (Pages 12-13)

1) The boy in the poems is <u>lost</u> in a "lonely fen".
2) The boy is <u>helpless</u> on his own and there is a strong sense of <u>danger</u>
   — "The mire was deep, and the child did weep".
3) He is <u>rescued</u> when <u>God</u> appears, "like his father in white".
4) Blake uses the story to make a religious point — he says we're <u>lost without God</u>.

Danger can come from People's <u>Violence</u> and <u>Aggression</u>

<u>The Field-Mouse</u> (Pages 60-61)

1) In this poem, the poet worries about the <u>violence</u> going on in former-Yugoslavia. She dreams
   about a <u>similar conflict</u> happening in her <u>own country</u> and how it would affect her family.
2) She dreams that her <u>home</u> is part of a <u>battleground</u> — "the air / stammering with gunfire".
   In her dream, her neighbour becomes her <u>enemy</u>, "wounding my land with stones".
3) She's particularly frightened by how <u>vulnerable</u> her <u>children</u> would be in a conflict.
   She dreams they "<u>dance in grass</u>" as the <u>gunfire</u> goes on around them.

Danger can be in the <u>Imagination</u>

<u>Death of a Naturalist</u> (Pages 42-43)

1) In this poem, a <u>boy</u> becomes fascinated with a place where <u>wildlife</u> has gathered around
   some rotting flax in a stream. He <u>takes frogspawn away</u> from the dam to show at school.
2) One day, the boy goes to the dam and finds it full of frogs. He's <u>frightened</u> by the <u>frogs</u>.
   He thinks they're <u>horrible</u> — "gross-bellied" with "loose necks".
3) The boy thinks the frogs are <u>violent and threatening</u> — they look like "grenades" and sound like
   "obscene threats". He thinks they want some kind of revenge on him, for taking away the frogspawn.
4) In his fear, the boy runs away. His childish imagination believes that if he dipped his hand in the water
   "the spawn would clutch it". The <u>danger</u> in this poem is mostly <u>in the character's imagination</u>.

Be afraid, be very afraid...

This is a bit of a grim topic — people being frightened and getting hurt. If you want more
of this doleful stuff, then read: 'Storm on the Island' (p.48-49), 'On the Train' (p.64-65)
and 'Cold Knap Lake' (p.66-67).

Attitudes Towards Other People

Poems are often about the poet's or narrator's attitudes and feelings towards other people. Sometimes their attitude towards others is very nice, and sometimes it's, erm, not...

> 1) Some poets write about <u>positive</u> attitudes and feelings towards other people.
> 2) Some poets write about <u>negative or violent</u> attitudes towards other people.
> 3) Sometimes a poet writes about <u>conflicting</u> or <u>uncertain</u> attitudes towards others.

Poems can show Positive Attitudes Towards Others

Digging (Pages 44-45)

1) The poet watches his father digging in the garden, and it reminds him of his <u>father</u> digging potatoes twenty years before, and his <u>grandfather</u> cutting turf.
2) The poet's <u>attitude</u> to his father and grandfather is one of <u>pride</u> and <u>respect</u>. For example, he exclaims, "By God, the old man could handle a spade. / Just like his old man". This shows that even now, looking back, he's still impressed by their power and skill.
3) He says that his grandfather, "cut more turf in a day / Than any other man on Toner's bog." This sounds like he's <u>boasting</u>, and shows how proud he is of his grandfather.

Poems can show Negative Attitudes Towards Others

Baby-sitting (Pages 54-55)

1) In this poem, a <u>baby-sitter</u> describes her thoughts about the <u>baby</u> she is looking after.
2) Her <u>attitude</u> to the baby is one of <u>fear</u> and <u>distrust</u>. She describes the baby in a very cold, <u>detached</u> way: "she is fair; / She is a perfectly acceptable child".
3) The baby-sitter feels <u>inadequate</u> because she's not the baby's mother. She <u>worries</u> that if the baby wakes, she'll be upset because her mother's not there: "If she wakes / She will hate me".

"Mad, moi?"

The Laboratory (Pages 30-31)

1) The woman in the poem has a <u>really angry attitude</u> towards her <u>lover</u> and his <u>new mistress</u>. She thinks they've made a <u>fool</u> of her: "they laugh, laugh at me".
2) She wants <u>revenge</u> and chooses to use poison to <u>kill</u> the mistress in a <u>painful way</u>: "Let death be felt and the proof remain". Through killing his mistress, she hopes to <u>hurt</u> her lover as well: "He is sure to remember her dying face!".
3) She is <u>excited</u> about the idea of killing and getting revenge. She has <u>no guilt</u> about what she is doing.

Poems sometimes show Mixed Feelings Towards Others

The Village Schoolmaster (Pages 28-29)

1) The narrator describes the <u>former schoolmaster</u> of a country village. The narrator's attitude towards the schoolmaster <u>isn't totally positive or negative</u>.
2) The narrator sometimes seems to <u>mock</u> the schoolmaster, e.g. he says that he didn't like losing an argument and would keep arguing "even though vanquished". But on the other hand, he also seems to have quite <u>fond memories</u> of the schoolmaster. He says he was "<u>kind</u>" and <u>loved learning</u>.
3) Overall, the narrator gives the impression that, although the schoolmaster had a bit of a <u>high opinion</u> of himself, he <u>wasn't a bad man</u>.

Anger, resentment, love, lust, hate, jealousy, contempt...

Poems which show characters' attitudes towards other people include: 'The Song of the Old Mother' (p.8-9), 'My Last Duchess' (p.22-23), 'Catrin' (p.52-53) and 'Follower' (p.50-51).

Love

There are a few poems on the good old-fashioned theme of love in this anthology, but <u>not many</u> of them are <u>romantic</u>. Some of them cover love of families, love of nature etc...

1) Some poets write about <u>romantic love</u>.
2) Poets also write about <u>loving their family and friends</u>.
3) Some poets write about their love of <u>nature</u>, or a particular <u>place</u> or <u>hobby</u>.

Some Poems are about <u>Romantic Love</u>

Sonnet 130 (Pages 20-21)

1) This poem is a <u>sonnet</u> (it's 14 lines long). Sonnet form is often used for <u>love poetry</u>.
2) In the first part of the poem, Shakespeare <u>goes against the reader's expectations</u> of a love sonnet. He's <u>pretty rude</u> about his mistress, e.g. he says her "eyes are nothing like the sun", her hair is like "black wires" and her breath "reeks".
3) On line 9, he says "I love to hear her speak". This is the <u>first hint</u> that he <u>does love his mistress</u>.
4) In the last two lines, the tone changes. Shakespeare says that his mistress is <u>just as wonderful</u> as <u>any woman</u> who's <u>praised</u> with <u>silly compliments</u>: "I think my love as rare / As any she belied with false compare".

Some Poems are about Loving your <u>Family</u>

Mali (Pages 56-57)

1) The poet remembers her <u>granddaughter's birth</u> and how it made her feel.
2) The birth of her granddaughter reminded her of the birth of her own daughter: "that unmistakable brim and tug of the tide / I'd thought was over."
3) The poet felt a <u>very strong love</u> for her granddaughter right from the start: "I'm hooked again, life-sentenced. / Even the sea could not draw me from her".

Some Poems are about Love of <u>Places</u> or <u>Nature</u>

Sonnet (Pages 34-35)

1) The poet describes how much he <u>loves the countryside</u> in <u>summer</u>.
2) He starts three lines with the phrase "<u>I love</u>", which emphasises his feelings.
3) He describes the countryside in a very <u>positive way</u>, using words like "beaming", "happy" and "bright" to show how much he likes it.

"Who cares about boys? I love shrubbery..."

Inversnaid (Pages 32-33)

1) The poet describes a place with <u>wild, natural scenery</u>, with a "darksome burn" rolling through the hills.
2) In the final stanza, the poet appeals for places like this to be left alone. He <u>loves</u> the "<u>wilderness</u>" and wants it to survive.

Some poets love Wolverhampton Wanderers...

The poems in this anthology are pretty bleak — even the poems about love tend to be a bit depressing. Other poems about love include: 'On my first Sonne' (p.6-7), 'The Affliction of Margaret' (p.10-11), 'Digging' (p.44-45) and 'Catrin' (p.52-53).

Memory

Many poems are based around memories — of <u>people</u>, <u>events</u> and <u>feelings</u>.

1) Memories can be <u>associated</u> with many <u>different feelings</u>, e.g. pride, shame, joy or anger.

2) People sometimes <u>block out bad memories</u>.

3) Memories can be <u>unreliable</u> — you might remember things differently to how they actually happened.

The Way we Remember Things Might Not be Accurate

Cold Knap Lake (Pages 66-67)

1) The poet remembers seeing her mother <u>revive a girl</u> who had <u>nearly drowned</u> in a <u>lake</u>.

2) The poet wonders if the memory is real: "<u>Was I there?</u>".

3) She describes the memory as if it is a <u>dramatic story</u>, with her mum as the "<u>heroine</u>". This makes it seem possible that the event has been <u>changed in her memory</u>, or perhaps <u>made up</u> altogether.

4) The poet uses the <u>lake</u> as a <u>metaphor for memory</u>. Things get lost in the lake (and her memory) which she can't find again: "All lost things lie under closing water / in that lake with the poor man's daughter".

My Last Duchess (Pages 22-23)

1) The narrator of the poem looks at a <u>painting of his dead wife</u> and describes what she was like.

2) The narrator's <u>memories</u> of his wife are <u>changed</u> by his feelings of <u>jealousy</u> and <u>anger</u>.

3) He says that his wife used to <u>smile and blush</u> at everyone, not just him:
"She had / A heart - how shall I say? - too soon made glad".

4) The narrator's <u>pride was hurt</u> by this. He thought his wife should give him all her attention, and ignore other men.

5) The narrator says he "gave commands; / Then all smiles stopped together".
This suggests that he <u>had his wife killed</u>.

Some Memories Inspire Pride or Affection

The Village Schoolmaster (Pages 28-29)

1) At the beginning of the poem, the narrator <u>points out</u> where the <u>old school</u> was in the village and starts describing what the <u>old schoolmaster</u> was like. It sounds as if the school <u>might be a ruin</u> now — "Beside yon straggling fence".

2) The narrator has some <u>amusing memories</u> of the schoolmaster, which suggests he was quite <u>fond of him</u>, even if he <u>didn't respect him</u>. For example, he says the schoolmaster would never give in in an argument — "even though vanquished, he could argue still".

Ulysses (Pages 26-27)

1) Ulysses has returned to his home of Ithaca after years spent away. He finds normal life <u>boring</u>, and wants to return to travelling and adventure.

2) Ulysses has <u>strong memories</u> of the <u>glory</u> of his former life. He remembers the "drunk delight of battle" and all that he has "seen and known".

3) In his past life, he became <u>famous</u> and took part in important <u>events</u>. He says, "I am a part of all that I have met".

4) He's <u>proud</u> of what he's done. Memories of his <u>past glory</u> inspire him to go travelling again — "I cannot rest from travel: I will drink / Life to the lees".

"Give me a sword and I'll show you a thing or two."

I remember it well...

Other poems which deal with memories include: 'The Affliction of Margaret' (p.10-11), 'Blackberry-Picking' (p.40-41), 'Death of a Naturalist' (p.42-43), 'Digging' (p.44-45) and 'Catrin' (p.52-53).

Politics

Politics is about how a country is run, and how a <u>government</u> treats its citizens.
Politics affects both <u>society</u> as a whole and <u>individual</u> people.

> 1) Politics can be about <u>conflict</u> and <u>peacemaking</u>.
> 2) Politics can be about the <u>differences</u> between <u>rich and poor</u>.
> 3) It can be about how <u>leaders</u> use and abuse their <u>power</u>.

Politics can be about *Conflict*

Storm on the Island (Pages 48-49)

1) The first eight letters of the poem's title spell <u>Stormont</u>.
   Stormont is the seat of <u>government</u> in <u>Northern Ireland</u>.
2) The poem uses a lot of <u>language</u> associated with <u>war and violence</u> to describe
   the storm, e.g. "Blast", "strafes" and "bombarded".
3) The <u>storm</u> battering the island is a <u>metaphor</u> for the <u>troubles</u> in Northern Ireland.

The Field-Mouse (Pages 60-61)

1) The poet describes spending a day <u>cutting hay</u> on her farm,
   while abroad <u>violent events</u> are happening in former-Yugoslavia.
2) She <u>tries to avoid the news</u>. She works "at the end of the meadow, / far from the
   radio's terrible news" and at the end of the day she "can't face the newspapers".
3) But even so, she can't help <u>thinking</u> about the <u>terrible events</u> that are happening.
   A wounded field-mouse reminds her of the <u>innocent victims</u> of the conflict.
4) She dreams about <u>civil war</u> happening in her <u>own country</u>
   — her neighbour turning against her and "wounding my land with stones".

Politics can be about *Peacemaking*

A Difficult Birth, Easter 1998 (Pages 58-59)

1) The title of the poem refers to the <u>Good Friday Agreement</u> of Easter 1998. This was a <u>peace
   agreement</u> which arranged for a new power-sharing assembly to be set up in Northern Ireland.
2) The poem uses the event of an <u>old ewe giving birth</u> as a <u>metaphor</u> for the <u>peace talks</u>.
3) The poet says they <u>didn't expect</u> the old ewe to give birth: "We thought her barren". There is a
   parallel with the peace talks — after such a long conflict, few people expected a happy outcome.
4) The birth is <u>difficult</u> and <u>drawn-out</u>. The poet describes helping — "We strain together, harder
   than we dared". This is a <u>metaphor</u> for how difficult the <u>peace talks</u> were.
5) The <u>ewe</u> successfully <u>gives birth</u> — a sign of new life and <u>hope</u>. This represents the <u>peace agreement</u>.

Politics affects *Individuals*

The Man He Killed (Pages 16-17)

1) A <u>soldier</u> talks about a <u>man he killed</u> in battle. He <u>didn't</u> have any <u>personal reason</u> for killing the man.
   He struggles to think of the reason he killed him: "because — / Because he was my foe".
2) The soldier imagines the other man was probably quite like him
   — joining up because he was <u>poor</u> and <u>needed a job</u>.
3) If it hadn't been for the war, the two men could have been <u>friends</u>.

Politics isn't just about the government at Whitehall...

Politics affects many areas of life: education, the legal system, healthcare, welfare, defence...
The Heaney / Clarke poems in the Anthology tend to focus on politics as a source of <u>conflict</u>.

Getting Older

People's personalities, outlook and capabilities often change as they get older.
<u>Adolescence</u> and <u>old age</u> are two important stages of life which poets often write about.

> 1) <u>Adolescence</u> can be a <u>difficult</u> and <u>emotional</u> time. This is the period when people start to become <u>independent</u> and learn to cope with life on their own.
>
> 2) <u>Old age</u> can also be a difficult period of life. The <u>approach of death</u> can make people think about what they want from the life they've got left.

Growing up is about Becoming Independent

Catrin (Pages 52-53)

1) The poet describes how she and her daughter have always wanted independence from each other. Even the <u>birth</u> felt like a <u>struggle for independence</u>: "to become / Separate".
2) At the same time there is a <u>strong bond</u> between the two of them, which makes the poet very <u>protective</u> of her daughter: "the tight / Red rope of love".
3) As her daughter grows up, she <u>continues the fight</u> to be independent of her mother, asking with a "Defiant glare" if she can "skate / In the dark, for one more hour".

Growing up can be Emotional and Difficult

Blackberry-Picking (Pages 40-41)

1) This poem is about the <u>disappointment</u> the poet felt during his childhood when the <u>blackberries</u> he picked <u>rotted</u>.
2) The first part of the poem describes his <u>childish delight</u> in the "glossy purple" blackberries. The second part shows his <u>disappointment</u> when they rotted: "I always felt like crying. It wasn't fair".
3) Gradually, as he grows up, he gets used to the fact that the blackberries are going to go rotten, and that <u>good things don't always last</u> — "Each year I hoped they'd keep, knew they would not".

They're only blackberries, Seamus.

Old Age can Motivate People to Get the Most Out of Life

Ulysses (Pages 26-27)

1) Ulysses was one of the great Greek heroes. In this poem, he has <u>grown old</u> and is living a <u>quiet life</u> on the island of Ithaca with his family. He's <u>bored</u> with life at home. Even though he is old he says he "cannot rest from travel", and seeks more <u>adventure and glory</u>.
2) Ulysses is aware that he is <u>getting older</u> and <u>not as strong</u> as he used to be, but he's still <u>ready for more adventures</u> — "Made weak by time and fate, but <u>strong in will</u>".
3) He <u>gathers his crew</u> and encourages them to join him in <u>one more voyage</u>. He says that even though they are old, "Some work of noble note, may yet be done".

October (Pages 62-63)

1) The poet goes to a <u>friend's funeral</u>. It makes her think about <u>her own approaching death</u>.
2) She doesn't want to feel defeated by death. Instead she decides to <u>keep on working</u> and writing as much as she can: "passing my death-day, winning ground."

This page is dedicated to Adrian Mole Aged 13 and 3/4...

Other poems about growing up and growing older are: 'The Song of the Old Mother' (p.8-9), 'Follower' (p.50-51) and 'Mali' (p.56-57). That's it for poets' ideas, attitudes and feelings. Phew.

Strong Emotions

Poets often show <u>strong emotions</u> in their poems — either their own emotions, or those of the people they are writing about. Strong emotions are things like <u>love</u>, <u>hate</u>, <u>anger</u>, <u>jealousy</u> and <u>joy</u>.

1) Poems are often about <u>personal</u> subjects, which the poet feels strong emotions about.

2) Poems about <u>difficult situations</u> often contain strong emotions, e.g. poems about death or danger.

3) Poets can show strong emotions through the <u>language they use</u> to write about a subject.

4) When a poet writes about strong emotions, it can make the reader think about times when they felt the same way. It often increases the <u>connection</u> the reader feels to the poem.

Poems about Difficult Situations show Strong Emotions

Mid-Term Break (Pages 46-47)

1) The poet describes going home from boarding school for his <u>young brother's funeral</u>.
2) He describes his <u>father crying</u>, even though in the past "He had always taken funerals in his stride".
3) His <u>mother</u> doesn't cry — she puts on a <u>brave face</u> for the "strangers" at the house. But her "angry tearless sighs" and the way she holds her son's hand, show how <u>upset</u> she is.
4) The language the poet uses to describe his brother's corpse is very <u>simple and effective</u>. It shows the <u>grief</u> and <u>shock</u> he feels.
5) He says his brother lay in his coffin, "as in his cot" — the contrast between a living boy in a cot, and a corpse in a coffin is <u>shocking and very sad</u>. The final line, "A four foot box, a foot for every year" also emphasises <u>how young</u> his brother was when he died.

Tichborne's Elegy (Pages 14-15)

1) This poem was written as the poet was <u>waiting for his execution</u> in the Tower of London.
2) The poet feels huge <u>sadness</u> and <u>bitterness</u> about his coming execution.
3) Throughout the poem, he keeps pointing out the <u>bitter irony</u> of his situation: even though he is young and healthy, his life is coming to an end: "My fruit is fallen, and yet my leaves are green".
4) He feels <u>angry</u> about the way his life is going to be <u>wasted</u>. Instead of being able to enjoy his life, it's going to be cut short: "My prime of youth is but a frost of cares".

On the Train (Pages 64-65)

1) The poet is travelling home on a train, as news comes through about a <u>terrible train crash</u>. She describes the crash as a "<u>blazing bone-ship</u>" which is a terrifying image.
2) She describes the <u>pain</u> of the <u>relatives and friends</u> of those killed in the crash. She imagines them trying to <u>phone their loved ones</u> and getting <u>no answer</u> — the "wolves howl into silent telephones".
3) The news of the crash makes the poet want to contact her own home and let her partner know she's safe.

Poets often write about things they're Passionate about

Inversnaid (Pages 32-33)

1) This poem is about a place in the <u>countryside</u> which the poet really loves, where a "<u>darksome burn</u>" rolls through the hills.
2) In the last stanza, the poet makes <u>pleas</u> for places like this to be left as they are: "What would the world be, once bereft / Of wet and of wildness? Let them be left".

Strong emotions are dramatic and compelling...

Poems are often about personal or dramatic events — no wonder they're emotional. 'On my first Sonne' (p.6-7) and 'The Field-Mouse' (p.60-61) are also good examples of this theme.

Use of First Person

If poets write in the first person, they use words like "I" and "me", rather than "she" and "him".

> 1) Writing in the first person allows the poet to use his/her voice directly.
> 2) This allows poets to talk about their personal thoughts and emotions.
> 3) The first person lets the reader see things from the poet or character's point of view.

Writing in the First Person can Express Personal Feelings

Baby-sitting (Pages 54-55)

1) This poem is about a baby-sitter's negative feelings towards the baby she is looking after.
2) The use of the first person means we hear the babysitter's thoughts directly.
   This gives her thoughts and feelings more impact.
3) Simple statements like "I don't love / This baby" and "I am afraid of her" are shocking because they are the opposite of how people usually think about children.

Yup, it's lovely out here.

Sonnet (Pages 34-35)

1) This poem is about how much the poet loves the countryside in summer.
2) Three lines of the poem start with "I love" which emphasises his feelings.

Digging (Pages 44-45)

1) The poet describes watching his father digging the garden and the feelings and thoughts he has. We hear his thoughts directly because he's writing in the first person.
2) He feels pride in his father and grandfather's skill at digging, and guilt that he hasn't followed their way of life — "I've no spade to follow men like them".
3) At the end of the poem, he finds a solution to this problem. He will follow his father and grandfather, but using his writer's pen as his tool, instead of a spade.

Writing in the First Person can be Persuasive

The Man He Killed (Pages 16-17)

1) This poem makes a point about the foolishness of war — how people who could be friends kill each other because they are on different sides.
2) Hardy writes in the first person from the point of view of a soldier who has fought in a war. This increases the impact of the message, because the character is speaking from personal experience.
3) Using the first person makes it sound as if the character is talking directly to the reader: "I shot him dead because — / Because he was my foe". This makes the poem more persuasive.

The Song of the Old Mother (Pages 8-9)

1) The message of the poem is about how difficult life is for many old people.
2) The poet writes in the first person, from the point of view of an old woman.
3) The character of the woman talks directly to the reader about her situation. She describes her list of chores, starting early "in the dawn" and not stopping till the "stars" are out. She contrasts this with the "idleness" of young people.
4) The poem gives a voice to a character who would usually be ignored.

The first person lets the poet speak directly to the reader...

'Tichborne's Elegy' (p.14-15) and 'On the Train' (p.64-65) also use the first person. It makes a big difference to the effect of a poem, as it lets the poet talk personally — poems like 'The Man He Killed' would lose a lot of impact if it was just "he" or "she" instead of "I".

Characters

Most poets write about people — apart from the nature-loving, obsessed-with-potatoes brigade.

1) Many poems are about particular characters — their <u>personality</u>, <u>actions</u> and <u>emotions</u>.
2) The characters in a poem can be <u>real</u> or completely <u>made-up</u>.
3) Sometimes the main character is the <u>poet</u> him/herself.
4) Sometimes important characters aren't actually present in the poem — they're just <u>talked about</u> by the narrator.

The Poet has an Opinion about the Characters

Catrin (Pages 52-53)

1) The poet describes her <u>daughter</u>, <u>Catrin</u>, as a <u>strong character</u>, who wants <u>independence</u> from her mother, e.g. she demands to be allowed to stay out late "In the dark, for one more hour".
2) The poet seems to have a <u>difficult relationship</u> with her daughter. She describes the birth as "our first / Fierce confrontation" — suggesting it was the first of many.
3) The poet describes her daughter as <u>beautiful</u> — "your straight, strong, long / Brown hair". But even this <u>admiration</u> is mixed with feelings of <u>conflict</u> — "your rosy, / Defiant glare".

Another poem about his Dad. What about me, huh?

Follower (Pages 50-51)

1) The poem is about the poet's relationship with his <u>father</u>.
2) The poet describes being a child following his <u>father</u> around the farm. He <u>admired</u> his father's strength and skill: "The horses strained at his clicking tongue. / An expert".
3) Now they are both older, their <u>relationship</u> is <u>reversed</u>: "today / It is my father who keeps stumbling / Behind me". The poet's view of his father has <u>changed</u>.

Sometimes a Key Character is Absent

The Affliction of Margaret (Pages 10-11)

1) In this poem, a woman called Margaret worries about what has happened to her son who disappeared seven years ago. Even though we <u>never meet the son</u>, he is an <u>important character</u> in the poem.
2) Margaret's opinion of her son is very <u>warm and positive</u>. She says that he was "among the prime in worth, / An object beauteous to behold".
3) There are hints though, that her son <u>wasn't perfect</u>. She says, "If things ensued that wanted grace, / As hath been said, they were not base". This suggests that other people didn't like his behaviour — but Margaret still defends him.
4) The fact that he's left his mother without word for seven years, suggests he <u>might not care about her</u>. The sadness of the poem comes from the fact that she still cares so much for him.

My Last Duchess (Pages 22-23)

1) In the poem, a rich man looks at a painting of his <u>dead wife</u>, and describes what she was like.
2) The <u>character</u> of the dead wife is described in a lot of detail — but all through the <u>eyes of her husband</u>, who <u>didn't trust</u> her. We never hear her side of the story.
3) The husband says his wife made him angry because she <u>smiled and blushed at everyone</u>, rather than just at him: "her looks went everywhere."

Characters are just the people in a poem...

Other poems with strong characters include: 'The Song of the Old Mother' (p.8-9), 'The Village Schoolmaster' (p.28-29), 'The Laboratory' (p.30-31) and 'Death of a Naturalist' (p.42-43).

Imagery

The way a poet writes can make you form a picture in your head of what's being described — this is called "imagery". Two common forms of imagery are <u>metaphors</u> and <u>similes</u> (see glossary).

> 1) Imagery helps the reader <u>imagine</u> the situations, characters and emotions described in a poem.
>
> 2) Imagery often uses <u>comparisons</u> to describe something, e.g. "She ran like the wind".

Some Images Appeal to our Emotions

The Field-Mouse (Pages 60-61)

1) In this poem, the poet spends the day <u>cutting hay</u> with her family, and worries about the <u>violence</u> going on abroad, in former-Yugoslavia.

2) The poet uses <u>war-like language</u> to describe the hay-cutting: "killed flowers", "the field lies bleeding", "the field's hurt". This imagery links the hay-cutting to the violence going on abroad.

3) She describes a "quivering mouse" hurt during the harvesting, which dies in her child's hands. This image is <u>very moving</u>: "It curls in agony big as itself / and the star goes out in its eye".

4) She dreams about her own children in a situation as violent as that in the former-Yugoslavia. She describes them as being as <u>vulnerable and breakable</u> as the field-mouse: "their bones brittle as mouse-ribs".

The rarely spotted metaphor-mouse

At a Potato Digging (Pages 36-37)

1) This poem describes both a <u>modern-day potato digging</u>, and the <u>Irish potato famine</u> in the 1840s.

2) <u>Bleak imagery</u> is used to describe the potato digging — the "ragged" line of people are like "crows attacking" the fields.

3) <u>Religious imagery</u> is also used to describe the digging — "Processional stooping through the turf". This emphasises how important the potato crop is. Without it, there is the <u>threat of famine</u>.

4) <u>Shocking imagery</u> is used to describe the <u>starving people</u> during the famine — "Mouths tightened in".

Poets use Imagery to Describe Places

Patrolling Barnegat (Pages 18-19)

1) The poet describes watchmen patrolling the beach during a <u>fierce storm</u>. He uses imagery to show how strong and frightening the storm is.

2) He describes the bad weather as if it is a <u>violent, attacking force</u> — e.g. "savagest trinity lashing".

3) The <u>sound of the gale</u> is described as if it's a <u>person's voice</u>: there's an "incessant undertone muttering" and sometimes it sounds like someone shrieking with "demoniac laughter".

4) He emphasises the <u>gloominess</u> of the scene with words like "midnight", "shadows" and "murk".

Inversnaid (Pages 32-33)

1) The poet describes a place he loves in the <u>countryside</u>. He appeals for wild, natural places to be left as they are.

2) He builds up an image of the "<u>darksome burn</u>" in the first three verses. He emphasises the <u>colours</u>: the river is "horseback brown", the lake "pitchblack" and the froth on the lake "fawn".

3) He also describes the <u>movement</u> of the place: the river "roaring down" to the lake, the froth "Turns and twindles" over the water and the brook "treads through" the hills.

Imagery is an important poetic device...

Most poems have a bit of imagery in. Examples you can look at include: 'Tichborne's Elegy' (p.14-15), 'Ulysses' (p.26-27), 'Sonnet' (p.34-35), 'Perch' (p.38-39), 'Death of a Naturalist' (p.42-43), 'Mali' (p.56-57), 'October (p.62-63) and 'On the Train' (p.64-65).

Closing Couplets

A closing couplet is the last 2 lines of a poem.

> 1) A closing couplet can sum up the poem as a whole.
>
> 2) A closing couplet can make a new or surprising point, giving the poem an unexpected conclusion.
>
> 3) Closing couplets can be set apart from the rest of the poem, and sometimes they rhyme.

Closing Couplets can Sum Up a Poem

Cold Knap Lake (Pages 66-67)

1) The closing couplet sums up the main issue of the poem.
2) The first 14 lines describe an incident she remembers from her childhood, when her mother saved a drowning girl from a lake. Then the poet wonders whether this really happened or not.
3) The last two lines say that we can't be sure whether distant memories are real or not — "All lost things lie under closing water".
4) This is the only rhyming couplet of the poem, bringing it to a neat conclusion.

Storm on the Island (Pages 48-49)

1) The poem describes the inhabitants of an island preparing for a great storm. There is no shelter on the island, and their houses are battered by the strong wind.
2) The final two lines sum up the idea of how strong and frightening the wind is even though it's invisible — "We are bombarded by the empty air".
3) The poet is quite philosophical in the final line: "Strange, it is a huge nothing that we fear".

And still the wonder grew.

The Village Schoolmaster (Pages 28-29)

1) The closing couplet seems to sum up the poem, by telling us how the villagers were baffled by how much the schoolmaster knew.
2) There is some uncertainty too. The phrase "and still the wonder grew" could mean that the villagers are impressed by the schoolmaster — but it also suggests that they found him strange.

Closing Couplets can be Surprising

Sonnet 130 (Pages 20-21)

1) Shakespeare seems to be criticising his mistress, but the last two lines show he does love her really.
2) The closing couplet surprises the reader. It makes us look at the rest of the poem in a different way.
3) His love seems more genuine because he knows she's not perfect — "I think my love as rare / As any she belied with false compare".

Follower (Pages 50-51)

1) The poet describes being a child, following his father around the farm. His father was strong and skilful and the poet looked up to him.
2) In the last two lines this situation is reversed. Now it is his father "who keeps stumbling / Behind me, and will not go away".

Closing couplets leave a lasting impression on the reader...

This is a tricky theme to write an essay on. Think about what the closing two lines add to the poem. Other poems with interesting closing couplets are: 'The Song of the Old Mother (p.8-9), 'Inversnaid' (p.32-33), 'A Difficult Birth, Easter 1998' (p.58-59) and 'October' (p.62-63).

Irony

Irony can be <u>funny</u>, but it can also be <u>tragic</u>.

> 1) It's ironic when <u>words</u> are used in a <u>sarcastic</u> or <u>comic</u> way to <u>imply the opposite</u> of what they normally mean. People often do this to draw attention to something being funny or odd.
>
> 2) It's ironic when there is a big <u>difference</u> between what people <u>expect or hope for</u> and <u>what actually happens</u>.

Sometimes the Whole Poem is Ironic

Tichborne's Elegy (Pages 14-15)

1) The <u>irony</u> in this poem is that even though the poet is still <u>young</u> and <u>healthy</u>, his life is <u>almost over</u> because he is about to be executed: "My youth is spent, and yet I am not old".

2) Tichborne <u>repeats</u> this idea throughout the poem, with each line making clear the <u>bitter irony</u> of his situation: "And now I live, and now my life is done".

The Village Schoolmaster (Pages 28-29)

1) The poet uses irony in his description of the schoolmaster. He uses it to show how the schoolmaster had a bit of a <u>high opinion</u> of himself.

2) He says things which sound at first like they're <u>praise</u>, but turn out to be <u>pretty sarcastic</u>. For example, he says that the schoolmaster was <u>skilful at arguing</u>, but then says this is because he'd <u>never stop</u> "even though vanquished". He also says the schoolmaster had "<u>many a joke</u>" but suggests these <u>weren't funny</u>, because the children had to pretend to laugh at them.

3) The poet implies that the "<u>rustics</u>" found the schoolmaster <u>impressive</u> because they <u>didn't understand him</u>. The things he said <u>sounded good</u> ("words of learned length and thundering sound") and so they <u>assumed</u> he must be really clever.

The Man He Killed (Pages 16-17)

1) The poet points out that the man he <u>shot dead</u> could have been his <u>friend</u> if they'd met in <u>different circumstances</u>.

2) It's <u>ironic</u> that, if they'd met "By some old ancient inn", rather than being lined up against each other across a battlefield, they would have been <u>having a drink</u> together instead of <u>shooting at each other</u>.

3) The irony in this poem is <u>pretty bitter</u>, for example when the narrator says "Yes; quaint and curious war is!". Although the poem uses irony, it's making a <u>serious point</u> about the waste and tragedy of war.

Irony Can Come Out at the End of the Poem

Follower (Pages 50-51)

1) The poet describes how he <u>followed</u> his father, the "expert" in ploughing.

2) The poet "stumbled in his hob-nailed wake" — he greatly <u>respected</u> his father and wanted to <u>be like him</u>.

3) At the end, the roles are <u>reversed</u> — "It is my father who keeps stumbling / Behind me". Ironically, his father, who he had always <u>worshipped</u>, is now a <u>nuisance</u> following him.

Isn't it ironic...

Other poems with a spot of irony include: 'Sonnet 130' (p.20-21), 'My Last Duchess' (p.22-23) and 'Death of a Naturalist' (p.42-43).

Language Effects

Language effects are the way the <u>sounds</u> of words in a poem are used to make a certain impression on the reader. Examples of language effects are <u>alliteration</u>, <u>rhyme</u>, <u>assonance</u> and <u>onomatopoeia</u>.

1) Language effects can create a <u>mood</u> or <u>atmosphere</u> in a poem.
2) Language effects can be useful for creating a <u>vivid picture</u> in the reader's mind of the <u>place</u> or <u>person</u> described in the poem.
3) Language effects can make a poet's <u>feelings</u> or <u>opinions</u> more forceful and convincing.

Language Effects Can be Used to Describe Nature

Perch (Pages 38-39)

1) The <u>alliteration</u> in "runty and ready" strengthens the <u>small</u> but <u>lively</u> impression we get of the perch.
2) <u>Assonance</u> of the words "grunts", "runty" and "bluntly" drives home the <u>ordinary appearance</u> of the fish.

Oink.

Inversnaid (Pages 32-33)

1) <u>Alliteration</u> in the phrase "rollrock highroad roaring" makes the reader think of the <u>roar</u> of the water flowing down over the <u>stony bed</u> of the stream.
2) The <u>alliteration</u> of "In coop and in comb" add to the impression of a <u>rugged setting</u>.
3) <u>Rhyming couplets</u> and a regular rhythm give the poem a <u>natural</u> and <u>attractive</u> feel.
4) In the last verse, the poet makes a point about how <u>important</u> it is to keep places like Inversnaid as they are. Repeating "w" sounds makes the poet's point more <u>effectively</u>, by reminding us of the <u>sounds of the countryside</u>, like the <u>wind</u> blowing around the hills.

Language Effects make Descriptions seem More Vivid

On the Train (Pages 64-65)

1) In the first four lines, <u>alliteration</u> suggests the <u>rhythm</u> of the <u>train journey</u>: "flooded fields", "rocking, rocking the rails", "black box", and "tea trembles".
2) In the last stanza, the poet uses <u>short sentences</u> and a <u>direct question</u> to show her <u>anxiety</u>: "I phone. No answer. Where are you now?".

At a Potato Digging (Pages 36-37)

1) Heaney uses <u>alliteration</u> to make his descriptions more <u>vivid</u>. For example, alliteration in the phrases "A higgledy line from hedge to headland" and "ragged ranks" creates an image of the potato diggers as a scattered band of people <u>working together</u>.
2) The poem also uses <u>repetition</u> of <u>distinctive words</u> to link different parts of the poem. For example, the line of modern-day potato diggers is described as "<u>higgledy</u>". Later in the poem, the starved bodies of the famine victims are described as "<u>higgledy</u> skeletons".

Language effects make descriptions more memorable...

Learn how to spell "alliteration" before your exam. And look in the glossary to find out what assonance is, if you can't remember. Other poems which use lots of language effects are: 'Patrolling Barnegat' (p.18-19), 'The Eagle' (p.24-25) and 'Sonnet' (p.34-35).

Stage 1 — Planning

Planning your answer is essential, if you want to write a good answer and get a top mark. You should spend a good ten minutes on planning. That leaves you fifty minutes for writing.

A Read the Question Carefully and Underline Key Words

1) Read the question you've chosen a couple of times. The question will usually ask you how the poems show/present/use/convey the theme. Underline the theme and any other important words.

2) You have to compare four poems altogether. The question will give you the titles of some or all of the poems that you have to write about. If the question gives you a choice about which poems to write about, make sure you pick poems which relate to the theme the question is on.

3) Look up the poems you're going to write about in the copy of the Anthology you are given in the exam. Bend the corner over on those pages, so that you can find them again quickly.

EXAMPLE QUESTION

They want you to compare the poems.

The theme of this question is attitude towards other people.

Question 1   Compare how attitudes towards other people are presented in *On my first Sonne* by Ben Jonson, *The Song of the Old Mother* by William Butler Yeats, *Catrin* by Gillian Clarke and one poem by Seamus Heaney.

Remember to compare the following in both parts of your answer:
• the feelings expressed in the poems
• the way the poets express these attitudes.

Refer to these two pointers throughout your answer.

B Spend 5-10 minutes Planning your Essay

Write a plan at the top of your answer paper — this will help you write a good essay. Just scribble stuff down, like in the example below. At the end of the exam, draw a neat line through your plan, so the examiner knows that it's rough work.

Plan - poems to write about: On my First Sonne, The Song of the Old Mother, Catrin, Follower

1) Intro - attitudes to other people	4) Catrin
2) First Sonne	Shows her daughter is strong-willed
Proud of his son	Also loves / respects her daughter
"best piece of poetrie"	5) Follower
3) Old Mother	Hero-worshipped his dad in the past
Says young people are lazy	Now sees him as a nuisance
Uses contrast of old woman / young people	6) Conclusion - preferred Catrin

---

Planning is the basis of a good essay...

Always write a plan. It'll help you get your ideas in order, and write a well-structured essay. Once you've got a plan, you know what you're going to write — it will give you confidence.

THIS IS A FLAP.
FOLD THIS PAGE OUT.

Sample Essay — Death

Here's an example of a two-part exam question — and how to answer it well...

Here's an Exam-style Question about Death

Question 1   You should answer both parts (a) and (b)

(a)   Compare how ideas about death are presented in *On my first Sonne* by Ben Jonson and one other poem from the Pre-1914 Poetry Bank.

(b)   Compare the ways poets present death in *Mid-Term Break* by Seamus Heaney and one poem by Gillian Clarke.

Remember to compare the following in your answer:
• the feelings about death described in the poems
• the language used to describe death.

Here's an Example of a Plan for this Answer

Plan – poems to write about: On my first Sonne, The Man He Killed, Mid-Term Break, October

PART (A)	PART (B)
1) Intro about theme – death	Intro
2) Man He Killed	4) Mid-Term
Seems strange to kill in war	Confused feelings
Conversational language – sounds like he's thinking about it	Seems uncomfortable at the funeral
3) First Sonne	5) October
Saddened by death but says maybe it's a good thing	feelings are clearer and more intense
Metaphorical lang – "fleshes rage"	Takes something positive out of death
Conc – preferred Man He Killed –	6) Conc – preferred 'October' –
seems most relevant today	positive response

Here's a 'C' Grade Answer to the Question

Intro. 1

(a) Death is an emotional subject. For many poets, it is connected to feelings of grief, sadness and loss, and this is the case in Ben Jonson's 'On my first Sonne'. However, death can also be puzzling, as in Thomas Hardy's 'The Man He Killed'.

Briefly discuss the theme in the introduction.

Poem 1 2

The feelings about death in 'The Man He Killed' are described in a fairly calm and philosophical way. The narrator in Hardy's poem, a soldier, thinks about another soldier he killed in battle. He says that it is strange that he killed a man he might have been friends with if they had met "By some old ancient inn". He adds to this by saying that the man may well have been similar to him, joining the army because he "Was out of work". The narrator seems confused by the subject of death. He concludes that it is "quaint and curious" that war makes you kill people just because you happen to be on different sides. This thoughtful language suggests he is trying to make some sense of death.

The key words from the question are highlighted in green.

Treat each part of the question, (a) and (b), like a mini-essay.

Sample Essay — Death

Poem 2

The feelings about death in 'On my first Sonne' seem more intense and personal than those in 'The Man He Killed'. The poet is grief-stricken about the death of his son: "Farewell, thou child of my right hand, and joy". Jonson then goes on to ask "why / Will man lament the state he should envie?", meaning death. The poet uses harsh language to describe getting old, such as having to put up with "worlds, and fleshes rage", suggesting that death is better than life. So, in this way, Jonson's poem shows that death can be a good thing, because he sees life as painful.

③

Compare Poem 2 with Poem 1.

Back up your points with quotes from the poem.

Conc.

Hardy and Jonson describe different experiences of death. Whereas Hardy uses the story of a soldier who ponders on the strangeness of killing in war, Jonson presents a more emotional response to the death of his son. I find 'The Man He Killed' interesting, as Hardy's point about war seems appropriate at the moment, when so many people are still being killed in wars every day.

Include a conclusion for part (a).

Intro.

(b) The ways people react to death can be affected by their age. In Seamus Heaney's poem, 'Mid-Term Break', the poet remembers how confused he was as a child at the funeral of his young brother. Gillian Clarke's poem, 'October', on the other hand, shows how the death of a friend as an adult can make people think about their own death.

The question's in two parts, so answer each part separately.

Poem 3

In 'Mid-Term Break', the narrator remembers his feelings about death as a child. The language has a matter-of-fact, descriptive feel. Apparently emotionless phrases like "In the porch I met my father crying" show that the poet remembers the funeral clearly, but, because he was only a child, was confused by it. The poet seems saddened by his brother's death, although he rarely says how he feels, possibly because he is too young to understand what is happening. He says he felt "embarrassed / By old men standing up to shake my hand" — he seems uncomfortable rather than grief-stricken by his brother's death.

④

Remember to use the pointers in the question.

Poem 4

In 'October', the poet's feelings about death are clearer than those in 'Mid-Term Break'. Clarke is saddened by the death of someone close to her, in this case her friend. The style of language in 'October' is generally more emotive than that in 'Mid-Term Break'. Harsh, depressing words such as "dead", "stony" and "weeping", show the grief the poet feels. The third verse, however, has an urgent, hurried feel. Words like "racing" and "running" show the poet's feeling that she must make the most out of life before her own death.

⑤

Try to write roughly the same amount for parts (a) and (b).

Conc.

These two poems show how death has differing effects on people at different stages of their life. As a child, Heaney did not understand death or how to react to it, whereas Clarke's response is intense and emotional. I find Clarke's poem especially moving, and I respect the way she takes something positive out of death.

⑥

Give a personal response in the conclusion.

Sample Essay — Imagery

Some questions will be about <u>poetic methods</u> e.g. imagery or use of the first person. Don't be scared off by these questions — you can still answer them using the six-step method (see page 85).

Here's an <u>Exam-style Question</u> about Imagery

Question 1   Compare the ways poets use imagery in four of the following poems.

Choose two poems from List A and two poems from List B.

List A	List B
Death of a Naturalist (Heaney)	*Sonnet* (Clare)
Follower (Heaney)	*The Eagle* (Tennyson)
The Field-Mouse (Clarke)	*The Song of the Old Mother* (Yeats)

Remember to compare the following in your answer:
• the effect of the imagery used in the poems
• how the poets use imagery to show feelings.

Here's an Example of a <u>Plan</u> for this Answer

<u>Plan</u> – poems to write about: Death of a Naturalist, The Field-Mouse, Sonnet, The Eagle

1) Intro about theme – imagery	4) Sonnet
2) Naturalist	Colours make images vivid
Descriptive, vivid imagery	Peaceful imagery echoes poet's happiness
Uses military words to show he feels frightened	5) Eagle
3) Field-Mouse	Imagery shows strength/height of eagle
Violent, painful imagery	Shows poet's admiration for eagle
Shows sympathy for people suffering from war	6) Conclusion – preferred Sonnet

Here's a <u>'C' Grade Answer</u> to the Question

Intro. 1   Imagery is the way poets use language to create vivid descriptions of situations, events and even emotions. In 'Death of a Naturalist' and 'The Field-Mouse', imagery is used to describe negative feelings and memories. In other poems such as 'Sonnet' by John Clare and Alfred Tennyson's 'The Eagle', imagery is used to show positive feelings.

Briefly introduce the theme and how it relates to the poems in your answer.

Poem 1 2   In 'Death of a Naturalist', Seamus Heaney uses imagery to describe his feelings as a child towards nature. The language is very descriptive, creating a vivid picture of the scene. The poet says "bluebottles / Wove a strong gauze of sound around the smell", and he seems to like it there. But in the second verse, he describes the point when he became repulsed by the frogs. He describes how "their loose necks pulsed like snails", creating a horrible image. A lot of the imagery uses military language, such as "Poised like mud grenades", and this explains why he felt frightened and ended up running away.

The key words in the question are highlighted in green.

You have to back up your points with good quotes from the poems.

Sample Essay — Imagery

Poem 2 ③

Gillian Clarke also uses violent imagery in her poem, 'The Field-Mouse', although this is connected to feelings of pain and sympathy for the victims of war, rather than disgust with nature, as in 'Death of a Naturalist'. In her nightmare, she describes "the air / stammering with gunfire", showing how terrified she feels. Another similarity with Heaney's poem is that Clarke also uses imagery related to nature. She describes how "the field lies bleeding", and this piece of imagery links the harvest to the theme of war. The description of how the mouse "curls in agony big as itself" shows how the poet feels sorry for its pain, and makes it a symbol for the suffering of those caught up in the war in former-Yugoslavia.

Explain the effect of the quotes you use.

Poem 3 ④

The imagery in 'Sonnet', however, is used to describe feelings of happiness, rather than fear and pain as in Heaney's and Clarke's poems. Like Heaney in 'Death of a Naturalist', Clare uses imagery to describe nature, although 'Sonnet' describes simpler and clearer feelings. He says "I love to see the wild flowers come again", which is a typical image of early summer. A lot of the imagery in this poem uses colours, such as "water lilies whiten", which gives a bright, natural feel to the poem. This emphasises why the poet loves the summer so much. Clare also describes gentle movement, such as "the flower head swings". This adds to the peaceful feel of the scene, reflecting the poet's happiness.

Show how the poems are similar or different by using words like "similarly" or "in contrast".

Talk about how the poets use the theme to show feelings and attitudes.

Poem 4 ⑤

Like the previous three poems that I have discussed, 'The Eagle' contains a lot of natural imagery, but Tennyson uses it to show positive feelings, making this poem more like Clare's poem than Heaney's or Clarke's. However, while Clare describes how happy a peaceful summer scene makes him feel, Tennyson shows his admiration for the power of an eagle. He describes the eagle as "Close to the sun", which shows that he is very high up as he stands on the cliff. The phrase "mountain walls" creates the impression that the eagle is the owner of a massive house made out of the cliffs. When the eagle swoops down to catch his prey, the poet describes him as "like a thunderbolt", bringing home the amazing speed of the eagle. All these pieces of imagery create an impressive, powerful image.

Be careful to leave time to write about all four poems.

Conclusion ⑥

Imagery is important to the effect of all four of these poems. In 'Death of a Naturalist' and 'The Field-Mouse', the poets use imagery to describe feelings of horror and pain, whereas, in 'Sonnet' and 'The Eagle', the poets describe positive, natural images. One similarity between all four poems is that each contains imagery related to nature. I particularly like the imagery in 'The Eagle' as I find the eagle's speed and strength striking and impressive.

Always put in a conclusion.

Sample Essay — Characters

Read through this sample essay for some <u>handy tips</u> on how to write a fantastic essay.
<u>Key words</u> have been highlighted in green — both in the question and the answer.

Here's an Exam-style Question about Characters

> **Question 1** You should answer both parts (a) and (b)
>
> (a) Compare how poets portray characters in *Catrin* by Gillian Clarke and *Digging* by Seamus Heaney.
>
> (b) Compare the ways characters are presented in any two poems from the Pre-1914 Poetry Bank.
>
> Remember to compare the following in both parts of your answer:
> • the personalities of the characters in the poems
> • how the poets present the characters.

Here's an Example of a Plan for this Answer

Plan: poems to write about: Catrin, Digging, The Laboratory, The Village Schoolmaster

PART (A)	PART (B)
1) Intro about theme – characters	Intro to part (b)
2) Catrin	4) Lab
Character is defiant and aggressive	Obsessed with revenge
She is also strong and good-looking	We hear her voice directly
3) Digging	5) Schoolmaster
Poet admires his father's skill at digging	Frightening but skilful
Also proud of his grandfather	Villagers find him mysterious
Conclusion for part (a)	6) Conclusion for part (b)
Liked character of poet's father	Schoolmaster is more interesting character

Here's a 'C' Grade Answer to the Question

Intro. 1

(a) Characters are the people whose personalities, emotions or actions are portrayed in a poem. Poets use various techniques to portray their characters. In Gillian Clarke's poem 'Catrin', the poet describes her mixed feelings for her daughter, while, in 'Digging', Seamus Heaney shows the pride he feels for his father and grandfather.

Briefly discuss the theme in the introduction.

Poem 1 2

In 'Catrin', the poet's daughter, Catrin, has been a strong, defiant person all her life, and the language the poet uses to describe her shows this. The poet describes her birth as "our first / Fierce confrontation", and this unusual way of describing the event shows that the poet has always thought of this character as a difficult person to get on with. The impression of Catrin in the present day is the same as in the past, describing the "Defiant glare" she uses to try to get her own way. However, Clarke also loves and respects Catrin. Her "straight, strong, long / Brown hair" makes her seem a healthy and impressive character.

Talk about how the language in the poem gives a particular impression of the characters.

Sample Essay — Characters

Poem 2

3

In 'Digging', Seamus Heaney also has feelings of pride and admiration for the characters he describes, but they are more straightforward than those in 'Catrin'. Again, the language is important to showing the poet's feelings. He greatly admires his father, proudly telling us how "the old man could handle a spade". The poet is equally proud of his grandfather's digging skills. When he describes how he "cut more turf in a day / Than any other man on Toner's bog", it sounds like a proud boast. The poet's admiration is so strong that he sounds disappointed when he realises that he has "no spade to follow men like them". But he is determined to follow in the footsteps of these characters as best he can with his writing.

Compare the second poem with the first poem.

The key words from the question are highlighted in green.

Conclusion

Both 'Catrin' and 'Digging' describe strong emotions for family members. Clarke describes her mixed feelings of love and frustration for her strong, defiant daughter, while Heaney admiringly remembers his strong, hard-working ancestors. I find the character of the father in 'Digging' particularly interesting, as the down-to-earth picture of "his straining rump among the flowerbeds" creates a vivid picture of him.

Include a conclusion for part (a).

Intro.

(b) Poets can present characters in straightforward or more complicated ways. In 'The Laboratory', the poet describes a character who is determined to get revenge on her unfaithful lover. The character described in 'The Village Schoolmaster', on the other hand, is less clear-cut, as the poet gives a confusing impression of him.

The question's in two parts, so answer each part separately.

Poem 3

4

In 'The Laboratory', the poet presents the main character as obsessed with getting revenge on her lover by poisoning his mistress. She plans to murder her rival and does not seem to care about right or wrong. She says, "He is sure to remember her dying face!", suggesting she takes pleasure from the horrific details of the murder. We get an idea of the narrator's deranged state of mind, because we hear her voice directly.

Remember to use the pointers in the question.

Poem 4

5

In contrast, the character described in Oliver Goldsmith's poem, 'The Village Schoolmaster', seems more mysterious. The language the poet uses to describe the schoolmaster gives us an uncertain and contradictory idea of what he was like. On the one hand, he was "A man severe", who children were so frightened of they pretended to laugh at his jokes. But the narrator also tells us, "he was kind", and there is a tone of admiration as we are told of all his knowledge and skills. The phrase that seems to sum up the schoolmaster is "still the wonder grew". We do not know what to make of him, as, unlike the woman in 'The Laboratory', whose strong feelings are clear, the description of the schoolmaster is uncertain.

Try to write roughly the same amount for parts (a) and (b).

Back up your points with quotes from the poem.

Conclusion

6

Two very different characters are described in 'The Laboratory' and 'The Village Schoolmaster'. Browning's poem is about a violent and vengeful character, whereas Goldsmith portrays an odd, mysterious character. I find the schoolmaster intriguing, as he seems to be a rather contradictory character, and the descriptions of him could be interpreted in different ways.

Give a personal response in the conclusion.

Glossary

adjective	A word that <u>describes</u> something, e.g. "big", "fast", "annoying".
alliteration	Where words <u>start</u> with the <u>same letter</u>. It's often used in poetry to give a nice pattern to a phrase. E.g. 'S̲ally's s̲lipper s̲lipped on a s̲limy s̲lug.'
ambiguity	Where a word or phrase has <u>two or more</u> possible <u>meanings</u>.
assonance	When words share the same vowel sound but the consonants are different. E.g. "L̲i̲sa had a p̲ie̲ce of ch̲ee̲se before sh̲e̲ went to sl̲ee̲p, to help her dr̲ea̲m."
blank verse	Poetry that <u>doesn't rhyme</u>, usually in <u>iambic pentameters</u>.
colloquial	Sounding like everyday <u>spoken</u> language.
compound word	A word that is made up of two or more other words <u>put together</u>, e.g. "flame-red".
consonants	All the letters in the alphabet that <u>aren't vowels</u>.
contrast	When two things are described in a way which emphasises <u>how different</u> they are. E.g. a poet might contrast two different places or two different people.
dialect	<u>Regional variation</u> of a <u>language</u>. People from different places might use different words or sentence constructions. E.g. In some northern English dialects, people might say "Ey up" instead of "Hello".
empathy	When someone feels like they <u>understand</u> what someone else is experiencing and how they <u>feel</u> about it.
enjambement	When a sentence runs over from <u>one line</u> to the <u>next</u>.
iambic pentameter	This is a form of poetry that doesn't rhyme, but usually has a clear <u>metre</u> of <u>ten syllables</u> — five of them stressed, and five unstressed. The <u>stress</u> falls on <u>every second syllable</u>, e.g. "Co̲ral is f̲ar more r̲ed than h̲er lips' r̲ed."
imagery	Language that creates a <u>picture in your mind</u>.
irony	When <u>words</u> are used in a <u>sarcastic</u> or <u>comic</u> way to <u>imply the opposite</u> of what they normally mean. It can also mean when there is a big difference between <u>what people expect</u> and <u>what actually happens</u>.
language	The <u>choice of words</u> used. The language determines the effect the piece of writing will have on the reader, e.g. it can be emotive or persuasive.
layout	The way a piece of poetry is visually <u>presented</u> to the reader. E.g. line length, whether the poem is broken up into different stanzas, whether lines are arranged regularly or create some kind of visual pattern.
metaphor	A way of describing something by saying that it <u>is something else</u>, to create a vivid image. E.g. "His eyes were deep, black, oily pools."
metre	The arrangement of syllables to create <u>rhythm</u> in a line of poetry.
mood	The <u>feel</u> or <u>atmosphere</u> of a poem, e.g. humorous, threatening, eerie.
mythology	A collection of very old <u>stories</u>, often involving gods and heroes. Different cultures have their own mythologies.
narrator	The <u>voice</u> speaking the words that you're reading. E.g. a poem could be written from the point of view of a young child, which means the young child is the poem's narrator.

Glossary

noun	A word for a <u>place</u>, <u>person</u> or <u>thing</u>, e.g. "tree", "air", "Boris", "London".
onomatopoeia	A word that <u>sounds like</u> the thing it's describing. E.g. "buzz", "crunch", "bang", "pop", "ding".
persona	A <u>fictional character</u> or <u>identity</u> adopted by a poet. Poets often create a persona so they can describe things from a different person's <u>point of view</u>, e.g. a male poet might use a female persona.
personification	A special kind of metaphor where you write about something as if it's a <u>person</u> with thoughts and feelings. E.g. "The sea growled hungrily."
phonetic spelling	When words are <u>spelt</u> as they <u>sound</u> rather than with their usual spelling. It's often used to show that someone's speaking with a certain <u>accent</u>.
rhyme scheme	A regular <u>system</u> of rhyming words in a poem, e.g. in 'The Man He Killed', the 1st line of each verse rhymes with the 3rd, and the 2nd rhymes with the 4th.
rhyming couplet	A pair of lines that are next to each other and whose final words <u>rhyme</u>.
rhythm	When sentences or lines have a <u>regular fixed pattern</u> of syllables.
simile	A way of describing something by <u>comparing</u> it to something else, usually by using the words "like" or "as". E.g. "He was as pale as the moon," or "Her hair was like a bird's nest."
sonnet	A type of poem with <u>fourteen lines</u>, and usually following a <u>clear rhyme pattern</u>. There are different popular patterns for sonnets. They will often have ten syllables a line, and end with a rhyming couplet.
stanza	A <u>group of lines</u> in a poem that often share the same rhythm pattern and have similar line lengths. Stanzas can also be called <u>verses</u>.
stereotype	An inaccurate, <u>generalised</u> view of a particular <u>group of people</u>. E.g. A stereotype of football fans might be that they're all hooligans.
structure	The <u>order</u> and arrangement of a piece of writing. E.g. how the poem begins, develops and ends, whether it uses verses or not, whether it has a particular layout, etc.
syllable	A single <u>unit of sound</u> within a word. E.g. "all" has one syllable, "always" has two and "establishmentarianism" has nine.
symbolism	When an object <u>stands for something else</u>. E.g. a candle might be a symbol of hope, or a dying flower could symbolise the end of a relationship.
syntax	The way a sentence is put together so that it <u>makes sense</u>.
theme	An <u>idea</u> or <u>topic</u> that's important in a piece of writing. E.g. a poem could be based on the theme of friendship.
verb	A word that describes something you <u>do</u>, e.g. "run", "talk", "hope".
vocabulary	All the <u>words</u> used in a piece of writing.
voice	The <u>personality</u> narrating the poem. Poems are usually written either using the poet's voice, as if they're speaking to you <u>directly</u>, or the voice of a <u>character</u>, e.g. an elderly man, or a horse.
vowels	Simple — the letters 'a', 'e', 'i', 'o' and 'u'.

Index

Index

The Publisher would like to thank:

Poets:

Gillian Clarke 'October', 'Baby-sitting', 'Mali', 'Cold Knap Lake' and 'Catrin' from *Collected Poems* (1997); 'A Difficult Birth' and 'The Field-Mouse' from *Fivefields* (1998); 'On the Train' from *Making the beds for the dead* (2004), all reprinted by permission of the publishers, Carcanet Press Ltd.

Seamus Heaney 'Storm on the Island', 'Blackberry-Picking', 'Death of a Naturalist', 'Digging', 'Mid-Term Break', 'Follower' and 'At a Potato Digging' from *Death of a Naturalist* (1966); 'Perch' from *Electric Light* (2001), all reprinted by permission of the publishers, Faber and Faber Ltd.

William Butler Yeats 'The Song of the Old Mother' published by permission of A.P. Watt Ltd. on behalf of Michael B. Yeats

Image sources:

Image of Gillian Clarke © photographer Jane Bown

Image of Seamus Heaney © photographer David Levenson/Getty Images

Images of Ben Jonson, William Wordsworth, William Blake, John Clare, Thomas Hardy, Walt Whitman, Robert Browning, Alfred Lord Tennyson and Oliver Goldsmith © Mary Evans Picture Library

Images of William Butler Yeats and Gerard Manley Hopkins © National Portrait Gallery, London

Image of William Shakespeare © Royal Shakespeare Company

Every effort has been made to locate copyright holders and obtain permission to reproduce poems and images. For those poems and images where it has been difficult to trace the originator of the work, we would be grateful for information. If any copyright holder would like us to make an amendment to the acknowledgements, please notify us and we will gladly update the book at the next reprint. Thank you.